alt fiber

alt

25+ projects for knitting green

fiber

with bamboo, soy, hemp, and more

TEN SPEED PRESS
Berkeley | Toronto

Shannon Okey

photography by sasha gulish

Copyright © 2008 by Shannon Okey
Photography copyright © 2008 by Sasha Gulish
Photographs on pages 1, 3, 5, 9, 11, 13–17, and 25 copyright © 2008
   by Christine Okey
Front and back cover images by Sasha Gulish

Foxfibre® is a registered trademark of Vreseis Ltd. Ingeo™ is a
trademark of NatureWorks LLC. Soysilk® is a registered trademark of
South West Trading Company. SeaCell® is a registered trademark of
smartfibers AG. Tencel® is a registered trademark of Lenzing Fibers.

Ten Speed Press
PO Box 7123
Berkeley, California 94707
www.tenspeed.com

Distributed in Australia by Simon and Schuster Australia, in Canada
by Ten Speed Press Canada, in New Zealand by Southern Publishers
Group, in South Africa by Real Books, and in the United Kingdom
and Europe by Publishers Group UK.

Cover and text design: Katy Brown
Prop and fashion styling: Peggi Jeung

Hair and makeup: Meaganne McCandess
Photography assistance: Aubrey Trinnaman and Kelsie Wilson
Models: Ashley Brewer, Nancy Deane, Natalie Zee Drieu, Lynn Kysh,
Jennifer Pellecchia, Kelsie Wilson, and Lulu the Wonder Dog

Special thanks to Recchiuti Confections for allowing us to photograph
in their San Francisco Ferry Building Marketplace shop.

Library of Congress Cataloging-in-Publication Data
Okey, Shannon, 1975–
   Alt fiber : 25+ projects for knitting green with bamboo, soy, hemp,
and more / Shannon Okey.
      p. cm.
   Includes bibliographical references and index.
   Summary: "More than twenty-five clothing, accessories, and
housewares projects to knit and crochet using environmentally
friendly plant fibers"—Provided by publisher.
      ISBN-13: 978-1-58008-915-9
      ISBN-10: 1-58008-915-1
   1. Knitting—Patterns. 2. Plant fibers I. Title. II. Title: Alternative fiber.
   TT825.O3776 2008
   746.43'2041—dc22

                                                2008009386

Printed in China on recycled paper (50% PCW)
First printing, 2008

1 2 3 4 5 6 7 8 9 10 — 12 11 10 09 08

dedication

To Amy R. Singer, fiber enabler and friend, for her tireless promotion of these extraordinary fibers and her service to knitters everywhere through Knitty.com, and to Jonelle Raffino, without whom we probably wouldn't have had so many of these fibers to enjoy in the first place!

contents

ix **ACKNOWLEDGMENTS**

I **INTRODUCTION:**

knitting green with plant fibers

23 Linen-Times-Two Skirt

27 Rose Kilim Sweater

30 Audrey Swing Coat

35 Avery Jacket

41 Fern Tee

43 Bow Tank

45 Bamboo Cardigan Trio

51 Pure Cables Cardigan Set

57 Midnight Lace Stole

64 Merian Wrap

66 Sea Creature Möbius Necklet

69 Phoenix Quick Wrap

70   Summer Pine Shawl

72   Sjaal Scarf

75   Love-Squared Gauntlets

78   Dutch Girl Headscarf

80   De Fleur Socks

86   Sunny-Side-Up Socks

89   Zenluv Socks

92   Clever Socks

95   Kenaf Spike-Stitch Bag

99   Fuji Table Set

101   Irish Rose Bolster

104   Hemp Facecloth

106   **RESOURCE GUIDE**

110   **ABOUT THE DESIGNERS**

113   **ABOUT THE AUTHOR**

115   **INDEX**

acknowledgments

First and foremost, I'd like to thank my editor, Julie Bennett, for making this book a reality. I truly appreciate her vision in bringing it to life, not to mention her hands-on approach to learning more about the source material during our whirlwind tour of alt fiber booths at the National Needle Arts Association show. My wonderful agent, Judy Heiblum, is also my number one conspirator in taking books from their place in my head to the glories of the printed page. Thanks, you two.

And to the designers, without whom I would surely lose my mind trying to knit twenty-five-plus items all by myself, my absolute strongest and most heartfelt thanks imaginable. You not only helped to create the lovely items contained within, but you also amused me, sent me chocolate (Jillian, I adore you), and kept my spirits high throughout the process. Andi Smith (the genius and voice of reason, not to mention encourager extraordinaire), Jillian Moreno (fairy knitmother with an amazing sense of timing, given that she always seems to send the aforementioned chocolate on a day when I've completely forgotten to eat lunch), Nikol Lohr, Laura Chau, Keri Williams, Emma Jane Hogbin, Tamara

Del Sonno, Amy Gumm, Kate Jackson, Sivia Harding, Julie Holetz, Kimberly Alderton, Amy O'Neill Houck, and Jenny Willey: you are all an inspiration. Thank you.

Only Tamas Jakab could support, amuse, and delight me as he does, even when I am on deadline and making absolutely no sense at all. "Al Gore and the Time"—what? And special thanks to Tamas for doing the production work on the photographs in the introduction.

My mother, Christine Okey, for responding to these kinds of phone calls: "Ummm, I need to do a studio shot of about twenty things; can you bring the lights over this weekend?" She did the photographs in my first book and has gotten roped into pretty much all of them since. Poor Mommy. Thanks!

To the Fiber League, who understand what it takes to put out a book and who are always just a click away: Amy Singer, Jillian Moreno, Stefanie Japel, Kim Werker, Amy Swenson, Cecily Keim, Amy O'Neill Houck, and Kristi Porter.

Thanks to Megan Engelmann and Heidi Massingill for holding down the fort at our shop, Stitch Cleveland, when I was tied up with book work.

introduction:

KNITTING GREEN WITH PLANT FIBERS

Unusual plant-based yarns, or what I call *alt fibers*, are an interesting and addictive addition to the knitter's arsenal. Why "alt" fibers? It's short for "alternative" and a play on the terminology used in early online Usenet newsgroup names. In many ways, these newsgroups were the predecessors to today's wide array of topic-specific blogs and websites, so if you enjoy reading knitblogs today, you have Usenet to thank!

Taking the reference a little bit further, while a *knitting* newsgroup might feature moderators who expect some decorum from online residents, the *alt.knitting* newsgroup would tend to be more "wild West" in its approach, lacking a fixed set of rules or guidelines. By extension, this book and its contents also want to break—or at least bend—all the rules when it comes to using extraordinary plant fibers in knitting and crochet.

Cotton is usually the first and only plant fiber knitters try, but there are so many new fibers to play with that trying cotton alone is like going to an all-you-can-eat buffet and only eating carrot sticks from the salad table. Let's take a look at a sampling of the fibers you'll encounter in this book.

Soy is transformed into a sensuously soft yarn that is virtually indistinguishable from its silkworm-generated counterpart and improves upon real silk in ease of care. But soy isn't the only plant used for both food and fiber—so is corn! Wood pulp is reborn as cellulose-based lyocell (brand name Tencel), a durable and soft fiber frequently incorporated into higher-end fabrics. Pineapple fiber yarn resembles linen: while it's hard wearing, after many washes, it becomes

as soft as silk yet retains its durability. Ramie, kenaf, flax, hemp—even yarn made from nettles!—it's a fiber wonderland out there.

An added advantage is that many of these fibers are more environmentally friendly than cotton. Growing cotton has its downside—a constant need for water that has created unfortunate environmental consequences around the world. In Kazakhstan, the Aral Sea has lost more than six miles of surface area along with its lively fishing industry to large-scale industrial farms that diverted the rivers feeding the sea to irrigate endless cotton fields. Today, most cotton is grown in China and the former Soviet Union. By contrast, soy and corn are two of the largest American crops, and North American manufacturers are experimenting with bamboo and other fast-growing fiber crops that don't require nearly as many agricultural inputs, such as chemical fertilizers and irrigation. Because I believe in making the choice to use fibers from eco-friendly sources wherever possible, the cotton used in this book is all organically grown.

Plant fiber yarns are also allergy friendly. Even if you're not allergic to wool or other animal fibers, chances are you know someone who is or perhaps you know someone with multiple chemical sensitivities. This book features several sections about natural dyes and naturally colored fibers that may inspire you to use them for these hard-to-knit-for friends.

There's a small learning curve with alt fibers, but once you've mastered a few basics, you'll be on your way to knitting projects that are allergy friendly, impressive, and socially responsible.

my history with alt fibers . . . or a seed is planted

I first encountered alt fibers a number of years ago when Jonelle Raffino, the founder of South West Trading Company, produced a booklet for spinners complete with fiber samples. I ordered some soy fiber from her online and quite literally fell in love with it. At the time, the only alt fiber yarns I could find locally were linen and some terribly scratchy hemp that seemed better suited for tying up packages than for knitting.

Jonelle's soy fiber (trade name SoySilk) was a revelation—it was not only softer than the other plant yarns I'd tried, but it was also shiny and beautiful. I'd struggled to find something cool I could knit for my best friend, Pamela, a vegan, using fibers she would appreciate and enjoy. The eventual project, a soy "purls" hat that looked more like the gleaming oyster-born kind than anything grown in the ground, was unlike anything I'd ever knitted before. Fortunately, I'd recently learned to spin, so I could make my own yarn from Jonelle's fiber without worrying about what was commercially available as yarn. Over time, I hunted down more fibers and yarns—bamboo, organic cotton, linen that didn't cut your hand like twine—and my alt fibers class was born.

This class, which I've taught everywhere from yarn shops to arboretums, drove me to research other fibers that fit the out-of-the-ordinary-plants-used-for-knitting description. Other knitters were taking notice, too. Long before the mainstream knitting magazines featured soy and bamboo as anything other than an oddity, Amy R. Singer, the founder of

Knitty.com and author of *No Sheep for You: Knit Happy with Cotton, Silk, Linen, Hemp, Bamboo and Other Delights* (Interweave Press, 2007) published an article by Julie Theaker called "Plant Freak" in a 2004 issue of Knitty. Amy herself is highly allergic to animal fibers of all kinds (I've seen what happens when she accidentally picks up a skein of alpaca!), so it seemed only natural that her magazine would feature plant fiber yarns alongside the more common wool and wool blends from its very inception. I'm certain that Knitty fans and other online knitters helped spread these fibers' popularity through their willingness to experiment and try new yarns.

As more and more alt fiber yarns came on the market, the question I was most frequently asked was, "What can you *do* with them?" My short and sarcastic answer was and is, "Just about everything." I realized, however, that these yarns have properties both good and bad that puzzle even the most experienced knitters. Are they warm like wool? Well, they can be if you knit them a certain way! How can I

compensate for their lack of stretch? Plan carefully and use the right stitch patterns! How do I care for the finished garments? Most alt fiber yarns are machine washable and can even be dried in the dryer! In fact, some of these yarns look better the more they're washed. Try saying that about wool! This book is in many ways a response to all the questions I've gotten and a chance to showcase what these yarns can do.

about this book

Not only do I want to introduce you to these fibers and inspire you to use them in your own projects, but I also want to explain where they come from, the environmental concerns, how to dye and alter them to suit your needs, and many other subjects you won't see tackled in the typical pattern book. You'll notice that the "Resource Guide" at the back of the book is considerably larger and more detailed than most. I want you to be able to find the materials you need now for the patterns but also the information you might want in future if you become as fond of these fibers as I am. And don't worry: the world wool market won't go out of business if we knit a few soy fiber hats!

yarn qualities

If you are accustomed to knitting with wool or wool blends, adjusting your knitting style to alt fiber yarns might take a little time and experimentation. For one thing, they are not nearly as elastic as wool yarns, and depending on how the yarn is constructed, you may encounter some unexpected behavior. Alt fiber sock yarns are one example: to make up for the lack of elasticity, most plant yarns meant for socks have elastic, Lycra, or another stretchy fiber as one of their components. The inherent incompatibility of these materials with alt fibers can cause splitting as you knit. Fiber in wool sock yarns, by contrast, sticks to itself and generally tends to encase any nylon or synthetic fibers included for durability.

If you are having problems with your yarn splitting, try using a different needle or point type, whether it's switching from bamboo to metal or from dull tips to pointy ones (or vice versa—everyone's knitting technique is slightly different, and that's okay). Many patterns in this book include yarn notes about the alt fiber yarns chosen for the design that will help you make good decisions in choosing the right needle, finishing methods, and other must-know details. Don't be frustrated if you are having trouble with a yarn! Your knitting style may dictate using another type of needle or knitting method for that particular fiber. Some Continental knitters, for example, find they pick right through a loosely spun alt fiber yarn. Try wrapping your stitches English/American style instead or tensioning the yarn differently.

Wool does have a singular advantage over alt fibers—flexibility and resilience. This is the reason most knitting teachers use wool yarn to teach new students. It is forgiving of mistakes and can be coaxed into the proper shape with the right blocking. Plant fibers are not quite so forgiving, but don't lose hope—there are ways to tame even the most stubborn plant fibers (yes, linen, I'm looking at you)! If you're an experienced knitter, no doubt you've had some projects that just would not fit or drape correctly. Let's discuss the general properties of most plant fibers and learn more about the botanical and mechanical reasons these plants behave the way they do as yarn.

Remember your high school biology lessons about cell structure and plants? If not, here's a refresher. Almost all plants need water to grow, and the long cells that move water around a plant are called *xylem*. In the case of fiber plants, removing the xylem structure and spinning it into thread yields what's called a *bast fiber*. They are some of the strongest natural fibers and have been used for tens of thousands of years. Linen (indigenous to Europe) and hemp (originally cultivated in China) are the two most common bast fibers you may have encountered as a knitter. Other bast fibers include yucca and agave and sometimes ramie. (The jury is out on classifying ramie, since its fibers are shorter and come from the leaf instead of the stem. It's an oddball.) When I teach my alt fibers class, I compare bast fiber plants to a piece of celery. The tough strings running through the center are like bast fibers, and the surrounding juicy bits are the parts of the stalk and plant that are discarded during processing.

Processing bast fibers is time-consuming and tough to do correctly. If you've ever wondered why linen yarn costs so much, the description of how it's processed in the upcoming section "Linen" should explain it. However, it's worth the time and money. Textiles made from linen are instant heirlooms, as they're virtually impossible to damage by washing and, in fact, improve with age. Bast fibers of all kinds hold up well to constant wear and use. Keep this in mind when choosing a knitting pattern—make sure it's something you'll want to wear for years, not just one season. Of course, you could always pull out the yarn and re-knit it, but better to think ahead!

Cotton, by contrast, comes from the seed hairs of the plant, contained inside the fluffy ball called a *boll*. For centuries, it has been selectively bred to produce only the longest and strongest fibers, and to produce more of them. This selective breeding helped turn cotton into a major cash crop. Milkweed, kapok, and some other seedpod-bearing plants also produce short-stapled (see sidebar on page 9) fibers that can be spun with a little effort, although not on a commercial scale. Look for more about these side-of-the-road fibers in the "Alt Fiber Handbook" section on page 7.

Most of the plant fibers featured in this book are either of the bast type or have been created by coagulating together natural plant materials using the same methods that create synthetic fibers. Corn fibers are created from the natural sugars of the plant. This is why you should never iron them, unless you want some not-very-tasty burnt sugar on your iron! Soy fibers are made from soy proteins. Seaweed-based fibers are made up of tiny algae particles and a type of lyocell cellulose base. The exact processes used to create these yarns are proprietary, closely guarded secrets, but for the most part they resemble the process used to create microfibers such as acrylic and polyester, albeit using plant materials instead of petroleum-based ones. Extremely thin strands of the future yarn are extruded from a machine and spun together to make a knitting-weight yarn.

choosing and knitting yarn the right way

Synthetic alt fiber yarns tend to be slightly less rigid than their bast counterparts and generally softer to knit with directly from the ball. Depending on the yarn's actual construction (is it an unplied single, a 2- or 3-ply, or cable spun?), it will behave differently as you knit it. Airy cable-spun bamboo yarn is perfect for summery tops or wraps. Dense, plied hemp yarns will create a durable, hard-wearing jacket or bag. Using an appropriate yarn for the project you have in mind is just as important as the yarn's material. For an in-depth breakdown of how yarns are fabricated, check out *The Knitter's Book of Yarn* by Clara Parkes (see the "Resource Guide" at the back of the book).

But picking the right yarn is just the beginning. Have you ever noticed how some yarns bias in one direction as you knit or look funny if you alternate knitting from the outside of the center-pull ball to the inside of the next when you switch skeins? More so than wool-based yarns, many alt fiber yarns have a definite "direction" to them. To ensure consistency, no matter how you wind or otherwise prepare your yarn for knitting, always knit from the same direction. In other words, if you wind yarn into a center-pull ball, always start from the outside—don't alternate from ball to ball on multiple-skein projects.

And speaking of center-pull balls: many of the more unusual yarns, particularly the hand-spun or rougher varieties (such as hand-spun kenaf and hemp bark), don't wind well with a ball winder. You may need to do these the old-fashioned way. Start by creating a loose figure-eight "butterfly" around your pointer and middle fingers, then bend it over gently and begin to coil strands around the center section to create a ball shape. Don't wind too tightly! You don't want to add any more tension than is necessary to form your ball.

If you are working with one of the finer-weight yarns, such as the pine ribbon seen on page 70, you can wind it with a ball winder, but don't pull from the center as you knit (most knitters do this with wool yarns, which is okay because the fiber has enough integrity and "stickiness" to stay in its cylindrical configuration as you knit from the inside of the ball out). Instead, draw from the outside of your center-pull ball. Again, consistency is the key.

For yarns that come in small ready-to-knit skeins (like many of the yarns used in the sock patterns here, for example), you can knit directly from the skein.

blocking and finishing alt fiber yarns

If your wool sweater is an inch too wide or narrow, it's easy to block it out after knitting. In fact, proper blocking is not only the fastest way to get your sweater to fit just the way you'd like it to, but also a way to give the knit surface you've been working on for weeks a clean, professional finish. Alt fibers also benefit from the right cleaning and blocking, but they react differently than wool does, and they also have a few unusual features you may never have encountered.

Many alt fiber yarns were first created for weavers more so than for knitters—Habu Textiles' finer-weight yarns immediately come to mind. There is no inherent difference in yarns designed for knitting and weaving outside of weight, except that many yarns designed for weaving are sold with sizing coating the fiber. *Sizing* is a means of protecting the yarn from the stresses of weaving on the loom. It stiffens the fiber and, to a knitter's hands, makes it feel rather crackly. You can wash the fiber before you knit it to remove the sizing, but in some cases, this isn't recommended. For example, the Summer Pine Shawl (page 70) is much easier to crochet when you start with the yarn as is and wash it after completing the project instead of before. The finer the yarn, the easier it is to knit or crochet if you leave the sizing in.

If you find an alt fiber yarn that interests you but don't like the way it feels in the skein, try knitting and washing a sample swatch. You may even want to wash it multiple times. Often, the swatched yarn will soften and become much more malleable to the touch. One way to think about this is to compare brand new, line-dried denim jeans (stiff, even a little scratchy) to those you've washed and dried in the dryer a few times. The washing and machine drying can make a world of difference. And if you make a large enough swatch, you can always use it as a washcloth later on! (Many alt fiber yarns, such as hemp and linen, make fantastic washcloths.)

yarn availability

Any list of companies offering alt fiber yarns—and even a list of the yarns themselves—will inevitably be incomplete by the time of this book's publication, since the list grows every day. From a few years ago, when South West Trading Company and Habu Textiles were the only games in town, to today, dozens of new alt fiber yarns have come on the scene. Check out the recommended companies in the "Resource Guide" at the back of the book; try searching online by fiber, using a reference such as Yarndex.com; or ask your friendly local yarn-shop owner.

alt fiber handbook

Wondering where these fibers come from? Want to do a background check? Here's everything you might want to know about the alt fibers used in this book and the slightly more unusual ones that you may want to seek out if you're a spinner or that you might reasonably expect to see in a yarn store someday. Times are changing fast. I never thought I'd see soy yarn in the big box stores or organic cotton being sold by the nation's oldest yarn company, but here we are. Get to know these fibery friends now so you can put them to use in the future.

ABACA

Abaca, also called Manila hemp, is a banana species native to the Philippines. Like several other alt fiber yarns, it has a history of being used for rope making. Occasionally, abaca can be found in knitting-appropriate weights through Habu Textiles and other vendors. Its durability makes it perfect for bags and home decor items.

BAMBOO

Bamboo is a fast-growing member of the grass family, widely grown commercially for landscaping, hardwood, and many other uses—such as knitting needles! There are thousands of varieties spread around the world. Like hemp, it is possible to grow a considerable amount of fiber in one season, as bamboo adds several inches a day to each stem, depending on the variety. Bamboo fabric and yarn is naturally antimicrobial, is hypoallergenic, and wicks away heat. Some sock yarn manufacturers have been adding it to wool sock yarn for that very purpose, and large chains such as Target have even begun stocking bamboo sheets, hosiery, and housewares.

CORN FIBER

Ingeo is the trade name for a synthetic biopolymer fiber made from corn. It is created using a multistep process of fermentation and separation that forms a resin that is then spun into fibers for creating cloth or yarn. Its particular molecular properties cause garments made of corn fiber to wick moisture away from the skin for extra comfort in humid, damp weather. Check out the Fern Tee (page 41) for a fashionable solution to your summer-heat woes.

FIQUE

Fique is from the pineapple family of plants and is grown in South America. It takes dye very well and is available in a broad range of bright colors. Fique is also known as cabuya and is often confused with agave. Fique was in widespread use among the indigenous peoples of South America before the Spanish conquest, and it spread with Dutch traders to Mauritius and beyond. Fique has been used to make everything from rope to bags, baskets, and shoes. It's considered the national fiber of Colombia.

HEMP

Hemp fiber has gotten a bad reputation: it's itchy, ugly, and only worn by patchouli-scented earth mamas. Stop right there—hemp has come a long way. It now offers all the durability that made it synonymous with "rope" for centuries but with a softer finish and much better color choices! You can only wear so many earth tones, after all. It's also one of the most environmentally friendly crops there is. Hemp requires little water to grow, does not deplete the soil, and has eight times the strength of cotton (great for knitting bags or anything else that might need to be durable). It dries faster than many other alt fiber yarns and is even UV resistant. Hemp bark, the outer portion of the plant, is used in the Fuji Table Set (page 99).

KENAF

Kenaf is an annual hibiscus plant and member of the mallow family, which also includes cotton and okra. Kenaf is tough and fibrous, resembling a very tall okra plant, with similar leaves and blossoms. It is native to the tropics and has been used for centuries as a source of fibers for rope, burlap cloth, bags, and twine. Kenaf is extremely environmentally friendly, richer in cellulose than wood, and as an annual crop, it does not contribute to forest depletion. Given the right moisture, nutrients, and plenty of sunlight, stalks can reach heights of twelve feet or more in 180 days. In the United States, kenaf grows best in warm climates, such as that in Texas.

Dry kenaf stalks are composed of two distinct fibers: bast and core. The bast fibers make up about 35 percent of the plant weight. The core is short, balsa wood–like fibers that make up the woody core of the stalk and represent about 65 percent of the plant weight. Chopping kenaf stalks separates the bast and core fibers. It then goes through a separation process similar to that used in linen production. Core fibers can be used to create newsprint and other paper materials, making kenaf a truly multipurpose plant, like hemp.

LINEN

If you love garage sales and thrift stores, chances are you've run across linen tablecloths that are over one hundred years old but still look better than the new cotton one you bought last week! Linen is an incredibly sturdy and stable fiber, derived from the beautiful blue-flowered flax plant, that only improves with age.

The following firsthand description of linen processing in Hungary comes courtesy of my boyfriend's mother, who spent many winters watching her sisters use hand-spun linen to embroider traditional designs. This took place less than fifty years ago! Families in her village grew flax during the summer. After all the plants were harvested, they would be stripped of their leaves and submerged under a heavy rock in a nearby stream. Each family had its own area and

kept an eye on its fibers as the *retting* process took place. When you hear "retting," think "rotting," because that's essentially what was happening. The nonbast portions of the plant were softening, rotting, and falling away from the useful fibers. Eventually, when the excess plant material dissolved, the stack of fibers was taken out of the water.

The next step, *scutching*, crushes the inner, woody core of the stems by repeatedly hitting them with a stick. Two types of fibers come from this process: the preferred, longer *line* fibers, and *tow*, which is considerably shorter and not as strong. Line fibers are then drawn through a heckling comb to align and prepare them for spinning. The long individual staple length of linen fiber is what makes it so durable.

LYOCELL

Lyocell (brand name Tencel) is produced from wood-pulp cellulose using a solvent spinning process that pushes the fibers through an extrusion mechanism to line them up for spinning, then recaptures the processing chemicals to purify and recycle them. Imagine a really, really high-tech spaghetti-manufacturing machine. This method is

STAPLE LENGTH

No, it doesn't refer to office supplies. "Staple length" is a spinning term used to denote the average length of a single fiber piece. For example, wool staple lengths vary by sheep breed from two to ten inches, with three or four inches being the norm. Staple length determines how an individual fiber can or should be spun. The shorter the staple length, the more twist the yarn requires to hold together. If you've ever watched a favorite pair of jeans wear right through at the knee or crotch, blame the cotton's short staple length. Once one strand breaks, a domino effect runs through the entire area around it.

environmentally friendly because it lacks significant by-products but also because it turns a previously discarded product into a valuable commodity used in high-end fabrics and yarns. Modal, a type of lyocell made specifically from beech trees, is exceptionally durable and soft.

NETTLE

Also known as allo or alloo, this fiber comes from a particular species of the giant stinging nettle, a perennial plant that grows in shaded areas of Nepal. Traditionally, Nepali villagers first chewed the plant to separate the bark from the stalk. The allo fibers are then cooked for several hours in ash to soften them and mixed with white clay to lighten their color.

ORGANIC COTTON

Why use organic cotton? Though the United States no longer produces the majority of the world's cotton (China and the former Soviet Union do), more than half the pesticides sprayed in the United States each year are applied to cotton crops, and new chemicals are constantly being developed to keep up with annually mutating pests. Cotton requires a lot of water to grow, as previously explained, and the run-off from cotton fields sprayed with chemicals contaminates groundwater supplies. Organic cotton is grown without pesticides, which is much better for both the environment and you. Think about it: Your skin is your largest organ. Do you really want pesticide residue sitting on it all day?

PINEAPPLE

Pineapple fiber is taken from leaf veins of the pineapple plant. It dyes well. See also *fique* on page 8.

RAMIE

Ramie is one of the oldest plant fibers in continuous use. More than two thousand years ago, before cotton was introduced, ramie was used for Chinese burial shrouds. Ramie's fiber is found in the stalk's bark, and the process of transforming ramie fiber into fabric is similar to manufacturing linen from flax. Ramie fiber is very fine and silklike, is naturally white in color, and has a high luster. It is resistant to bacteria and mildew, is extremely absorbent, and increases its strength when wet. Ramie dyes fairly easily, unlike some plant fibers, and can withstand high water temperatures during laundering.

SEACELL

SeaCell is one of the newest alt fibers on the scene and has some unique things to offer the intrepid knitter. As a synthetic cellulose fiber, its structure is not much different from that of soy, corn, or other alt fibers. But SeaCell fiber also contains trace vitamins and minerals from the seaweed used to make it. The German company that makes SeaCell—smartfiber AG—claims the seaweed extracts in the fiber promote production of molecules that heal skin inflammations. In alt fiber yarns now on the market, including Handmaiden's Sea Silk, SeaCell has generally been blended with silk to improve its hand, although it's lovely to spin by itself if you are a spinner.

SILK

Silk, though technically not a plant fiber per se (it's produced from mulberry leaves by silkworms), is often blended with alt fiber yarns to give it a better *hand*, or knitting texture. It's used in this book as a blended yarn, a pure yarn, and as a substitute for milkweed in the Merian Wrap (page 64).

SOY

The soybean plant is a legume native to East Asia and commonly used for both human and animal food. Soy fiber is made from materials left over during the soybean oil and tofu (soy curd) manufacturing process, which is similar to making dairy-based cheese. After the oil or milk has been extracted, further proteins are removed from the leftover beans. This liquefied protein becomes the long, continuous fibers that are then spun into yarn. As soft as "real" silk, with a shiny luster like pearls, soy is a joy to knit. SoySilk is a trademark of South West Trading Company, which introduced this fiber to the knitting world.

beyond alt . . . the really unusual stuff

Practicality dictated using commercially available yarns for the patterns in this book, but if you spin or know someone who does, there are other plant fibers just waiting in your backyard or along the side of the road for you! A particularly good reference is Carol Kroll's book *The Whole Craft of Spinning* (see the "Resource Guide" for details). Chapter 8

in particular contains considerable information on spinning alt fibers, including milkweed, cattail, dandelion fluff, and more. For a more basic introduction to spinning, check out my book, *Spin to Knit* (Interweave Press, 2006), and you'll be on your way to making your own alt fiber yarns from the ground up (literally!) in no time.

AGAVE / SISAL / SISAL HEMP

These are all names for fibers derived from various subspecies of the agave plant. Despite the term *sisal hemp*, it is not actually related to hemp at all. Agave fibers are widely used for durable carpeting and rope and also for spa products. Although not yet widely available in finer weights suitable for knitting, agave is second only to cotton in worldwide agricultural production. It resists deterioration, especially in seawater, is easily dyed, and has excellent exfoliating properties that would be wonderful in a knitted facecloth if you can find yardage.

AMERICAN NETTLE

Stinging nettle and other members of the nettle family have been used in paper and experimental textile making. The fiber is hairy and tough and was used to make bags for English soldiers during World War I. Wear gloves when picking nettles to prevent the stings or skin irritations its prickers can cause.

BANANA

Not just tasty, it's good for fiber, too! Banana fibers have been cultivated for textiles for many centuries in Japan, where the young shoots are harvested and then boiled in lye to prepare the fibers to make thread used in creating traditional *bashofu*, or banana cloth. In Nepal, the trunk is used instead, and these fibers form yarns used for high-end, hand-knotted rugs. Modern manufacturers are currently beginning to produce more banana cloth, particularly in Japan, to take advantage of the more than one billion pounds of stems and leaves thrown away annually from the fruit production trade.

Beware false banana fiber yarns on the market, often from online resellers of Nepali recycled sari silk yarns. When subject to testing, they frequently turn out to be overpriced polyester or another artificial fiber, according to Jonelle Raffino of South West Trading Company.

CATTAIL

Cattail fibers can also be spun, although their extremely short staple length (approximately $^3/_8$ inch) dictates blending them with another, longer-stapled fiber. This probably falls in the crazy experimental spinning category, if you're keeping track, but it might be a fun project to try with kids if you happen to live near a cattail swamp.

KAPOK

Kapok, also called the silk floss tree, forms small pods similar to milkweed, filled with silky white floss. It is more commonly used as a soft stuffing but has hand-spinning potential if blended with another longer-stapled spinning fiber. It is also sometimes called Java cotton.

MILK FIBER

Milk fiber is another synthetic fiber similar to soy fiber in that it is extruded from dairy proteins. This, like silk, falls in the not-quite-plant-fiber category but has been included because it is used to blend with other alt fiber yarns (for example, in South West Trading Company's Craft yarn and Silk Latte spinning fiber).

MILKWEED

Milkweed is a plant native to North America that produces pods filled with fluffy fiber (often called floss) at the end of each growing season. It grows freely on the side of the road. Early European settlers used milkweed to stuff mittens and other clothes worn close to the skin due to its softness and ready availability, and during World War II, milkweed floss was used as a substitute for kapok, down, and other insulating materials. Its pods are not the only useful portion of the plant; the stalk of some milkweed species can be transformed into a linenlike fiber for rope using similar retting methods. The ultrashort staple length of milkweed makes it impractical for commercial yarn spinning, but with care, it can be hand-spun either alone or partnered with another fiber. See the "Resource Guide" for a link to an article with patterns that use milkweed.

dyed in the . . . wool?
natural colors and dyeing alt fibers

How many times have you been compelled to purchase yarn just because it was a beautiful color? It's probably more often than you'd care to admit. Color is powerful. We're attracted to it both intellectually and on a deeper, more visceral level. If you believe the evolutionary biologists, we're actually pre-programmed to seek out certain colors and associate good things with them. (Don't try using that to explain your next post-LYS-shopping-spree credit card statement, though. Trust me.)

Wool and other protein fibers come in fairly straightforward colors direct from the animal—white, brownish gray, moorit, fawn, or black. Plant fibers, on the other hand, can be grown in a variety of shades and also dyed with various plants and chemicals. Dyeing your own alt fiber yarns was once necessary if you didn't want beige, beige, white, or beige (though, fortunately, a wider range of colors has come

on the market recently), but dyeing is also fun and another way to express yourself through your knitting. Whether you use natural plant dyes or chemical dyes, you can achieve a broad range of colors, from the most luscious strawberry reds to mossy greens, indigo blues, and juicy oranges, plus every imaginable color in between. And if you've experimented with dyeing wool, you'll learn that using natural or chemical dyes on plant fibers is actually quite different procedurally.

What's the plant equivalent of being "dyed in the wool"— "dyed in the plant"? No need for any dye at all when the plant itself produces its own color! Some strains of cotton produce their own coloring agent, in shades of green, fawn, and brown. Picture these two things in your mind's eye: a sheep and a cotton boll. I'm 99 percent certain that you've imagined both as white. Farmers and textile workers historically

DYED IN THE *WOOL*?

"Dyed in the wool" is a saying that, like so many others, has a logical explanation. In the days before ultraconcentrated chemical dyes, woolen yarns and fabrics that were dyed before spinning, while still in the fleece stage, often featured stronger, longer-lasting color than did threads that were dyed after spinning.

preferred lighter-colored wool and cotton because it was a better base for combining in a large dye batch. However, with so many existing environmental concerns about cotton (see "Organic Cotton," page 10), let alone the processes used to dye it, naturally colored cotton has made a comeback. Sally Vreseis Fox, who developed organically grown Foxfibre (see the "Resource Guide" for more information), has played a major role in popularizing these naturally colored strains.

The Lion Brand organic cotton yarn used in the Rose Kilim Sweater (page 27) comes in three shades—vanilla, almond, and bark. But other brands, including Foxfibre, also offer various shades of green and reddish-brown tones. An organic cotton–spinning fiber from the Little Barn (see the "Resource Guide" for more details) and Blue Sky Alpacas' naturally colored yarn are a pale, dusty green. To deepen the color of these or any other naturally colored cottons, heat it. If it's already yarn, carefully boil it in a large pot of water; if you're spinning it yourself, wait until it is yarn before the heat treatment. You can also use washing soda to change the pH of the water and further affect the

yarn's color. The "Resource Guide" entry for Foxfibre can point you to additional tips.

One step beyond actually growing your fiber to be the color you want is using natural dyestuffs. Traditionally, dyers guarded their secrets closely. For example, the production of Tyrian purple from shellfish in the ancient world was heavily restricted, and only royalty could wear the resulting color. For an excellent description of this and other ancient dyemaking, spinning, and weaving processes, see Elizabeth Wayland Barber's book *Women's Work: The First 20,000 Years* in the "Resource Guide." Expensive pigments, like spices, cost so much per ounce that only the wealthy could afford them anyway. But our crafty forebears would not be denied their greens, blues, yellows, and reds! They found local substitutes for the pricy imports and developed native color formulas instead.

The easiest colors to obtain, dye-wise, are browns and yellows. Half your supermarket produce section will produce one or the other. Want to experiment? Save up some yellow onion skins and boil them with a sturdy cotton yarn for a while. Blues and reds (and therefore greens and oranges, when mixed with yellow) were harder to come by and therefore more treasured. Indigo, a native of Southeast Asia, is considerably stronger than woad and other dye plants that produce blue. It also requires a long, specialized process to

extract its color—and don't even ask what dyers used for part of it. (Okay, okay—ask: urine, that's what; disgusting but true.) Madder root, which produces red, grows reliably, if well cared for, but slowly.

Faced with these obstacles, northern Europeans learned to gather local plants and lichens to obtain their preferred colors. Even today some traditional-style plaids and tweeds in the Scottish isles are dyed in the weavers' crofts using these materials. Karen Diadick Casselman's excellent book *Lichen Dyes: The New Source Book* (see the "Resource Guide") contains information on many of these dyes. Though truthfully,

after smelling lichen dyes in action, you might prefer something that requires urine instead! See my book *Spin to Knit* (Interweave Press, 2006) for photographs of the orchid purple I obtained from a lichen that grows on granite.

Fortunately, these days most natural dyes can be purchased in powder or liquid-extract form. To show you the wide range of possible colors available, I enlisted the help of Felicia Lo, the frequently dye-covered hands behind Sweet-Georgia Yarns, to dye blues, yellows, and greens. And I'll talk about the reds, purples, and oranges I obtained using plant dyes for the Rose Kilim Sweater (page 27).

Lac

Brazilwood

Madder root

Cochineal

Quebracho red

Sandalwood

Osage orange

we've got the blues
(and the greens and the yellows . . .)

Starting with skeins of both natural hemp and a 50/50 hemp/cotton yarn from Lanaknits/Hemp for Knitting, Felicia worked with a series of plant-based dyes that produce blues, yellows, and greens. All skeins except indigo-only ones were mordanted with tannin and aluminum sulphate.

overdyeing

Overdyeing is the easiest way to go about obtaining secondary colors such as greens and oranges. The weld-, osage-, and marigold-dyed yellows were dipped into the blue indigo dyebath to produce greens and also into an iron bath to change their tones. This method also works for combining yellows and reds to make oranges if you don't have dyeing material, such as annatto, that will make orange directly or if you want a different shade.

There's more information in the following section about each of the dyes used above, in case you decide to experiment. Check the "Resource Guide," too, for links to online information and further reading. Creating color from plants for plant yarns could be an entire book on its own, but this should get you started.

natural dyes and where they're from

Natural dyes have a long history that is intertwined with the production of textiles and the economy. Elizabeth Wayland Barber's book *Women's Work: The First 20,000 Years* (see the "Resource Guide" for details) is exceptional in pointing out just how important natural dyes and fibers have been to the human experience.

BLUES AND YELLOWS

Indigo is a plant native to Asia and Southeast Asia that has long been the preferred source of strong and lasting blue color, eventually taking the place of woad in Europe. Woad contains the same pigment as indigo, but in lesser amounts. When you think *Braveheart*, think woad—the Picts and other northern peoples may have painted their faces and bodies with woad before battle, although some modern researchers have disputed this fact. Woad's colorfastness and durability leave a lot to be desired compared to indigo, which is also more easily transported (it can be reduced and dried into a cake for shipping). Woad was the only source of blue dye in Europe until the sixteenth century, when indigo began to arrive with the development of trade routes. Indigo is not soluble in water, which makes it difficult to use, and it must be oxidized onto the fiber after undergoing a chemical change, traditionally using (as described above) urine and other materials.

Weld is a plant native to the Mediterranean countries and southwest Asia that produces a clear yellow color. It is

MORDANTING

Mordanting is a means of preparing fiber to accept color by soaking it in a solution of water and one of many different plant-, mineral-, or metal-derived powders. This pre-dyeing step creates stronger and more colorfast shades. Even the smallest difference in mordants or dyestuffs can create an entirely new shade, and different mordants are used for different types of fibers. For example, aluminum acetate is used for cellulose (plant-derived) fibers, while aluminum sulphate is more commonly used for protein (animal-derived) fibers, though, as shown in these photographs, when combined with tannin, a plant-derived mordant, it will also work on cellulose fibers. Some mordants are readily available in the spice section of your local grocery store, but for more unusual ones, such as aluminum acetate, see the "Resource Guide" for a listing of dye materials suppliers.

In the photos below, the darker, smaller skeins are hemp (left), which were originally a slightly deeper tan than the hemp/cotton blend (right). Felicia then did a set of skeins mordanted with aluminum acetate in the same dye progression.

100% hemp yarns dyed with both aluminum acetate and aluminum acetate plus tannin, creating different shades of color using the same yarn and dyestuffs.

From left to right (aluminum acetate mordant on hemp/cotton yarn): weld, osage, marigold, osage and iron, weld and iron, marigold and iron, marigold and indigo, weld and indigo, and osage and indigo.

also called dyer's rocket. The flowers are particularly fragrant, but it is the roots that are used for dye. There is some evidence that weld was in use before the first millennium C.E., longer than even madder or indigo! Like many traditional dyes, weld fell into disuse with the advent of cheaper chemical dyes.

Marigold dye is, of course, derived from the common marigold flower. You can make your own by soaking the flowers in water and heating them with the fiber—they'll produce a range of colors from yellow-green to orange depending on the mordants and other fiber preparation.

Osage orange is an orange dye that comes from the wood of a North American tree native to Texas, Oklahoma, and Arkansas, although it is widely naturalized elsewhere. The tree features grapefruit-sized, green, inedible fruit sometimes called monkey brains or monkey balls due to their appearance.

PINKS, PURPLES, AND OTHER RED SHADES

The Rose Kilim Sweater (page 27) was designed to highlight the wide range of pinks, purples, and reds obtainable with natural dyes. Red dyes are not limited to fabric and fiber—food and makeup also make use of natural dyes. For example, annatto and *uruku*, a Brazilian rainforest plant, are often used in lipstick. Aveda's hair formulas for redheads use madder to intensify color. Henna, another natural dye, is used for both *mehndi* (skin decorating) and hair dyeing. Dyers have long sought new and better sources of red dyes, and we have quite a few of them at our disposal, as you'll see in this pattern.

Madder root is just that, the root of the madder plant. It looks like any dried-up root until you chop it and soak it in water (several days in the blender with an occasional pulse here and there works fine). Then it becomes a soupy, herbal-smelling deep red liquid that produces madder rose and other shades of reds, orange-reds, and red-pinks, depending on the roots themselves, the mordants, and the processes used to extract the color.

Quebracho red is derived from a South American tree. This hardwood is ground to powder to produce its dye.

Annatto is a food coloring often used in Mexican foods (you'll sometimes find it labeled "achiote" in your local *supermercado*). It gives an appealing bright red color and an unusual spicy/bitter taste to foods. Annatto looks like orange-red buckwheat groats and should be ground in a coffee or spice grinder to bring out its full color potential.

Brazilwood is native to India, Malaysia, Sri Lanka, and, of course, Brazil. It produces a very purplish red, although depending on its preparation (the pH level of the solution and the mordant), it can also produce shades of orange-red and pink.

Sandalwood, native to Southeast Asia and the Pacific, produces a lovely dark orange as well as a fragrant oil used in perfumes.

Lac comes from tiny Southeast Asian insects that are dried and ground up to produce a very intense, strong magenta-red dye, as well as shellac.

Cochineal is derived from several insects of the same genus that are native to South America (and which were spread to other tropical climes after the Spanish conquistador period). The Aztec and Mayan peoples even paid tribute to their rulers with large bags of cochineal and dyed fiber!

how i got madder . . . with a happy result

To dye with the red-dyeing powders just described for the Rose Kilim Sweater, I mordanted Lion Brand organic cotton yarn with aluminum acetate and prepared the powdered forms of each dye in separate glass jars. The mordanting process is dead simple: just dissolve the powder in water, soak the yarns thoroughly, squeeze out the excess water, and keep the skeins damp in a plastic bag or container until you're ready to dye. Dissolving the dye powders and extracts works much the same way as making powdered drink mix, except don't add sugar!

I used all three of Lion Brand's available natural cotton color yarns (vanilla, almond, and bark) to get different shades of color using the same dye strength. After attempting to dye the skeins individually in glass jars, submerged in a larger pot designed for canning with a handle to lift out all the jars at once, I resorted to boiling the fibers individually with their dyes in a large enameled pot to ensure the color had soaked through each skein well. You can never have too much space for the yarn to move around!

Please note: before you immerse skeins for dyeing, you should make sure they are tied off thoroughly but loosely in multiple locations around each hank. Use the same kind of yarn to tie off, to make sure the dye gets through where you've tied. This will prevent tangling and the desire to pull out your hair if you ignore my advice! Also, you'll want to wash the skeins after they come out of the dye bath, and that's more difficult if you don't tie them.

When you're satisfied with the color absorption, remembering that the colors will be much lighter when dry, allow the skeins to cool down and give them a quick swish in warm water. Fill your washing machine with hot water and detergent, and then allow the skeins to soak for a few minutes before running them through a short wash cycle. Again, make sure each skein is tied in multiple locations so the skeins don't get tangled or caught on the agitator. Line or tumble dry. If you're using osage orange sawdust instead of extract, be sure to remove it before you wash all the skeins together, lest it get caught in the other skeins as well.

dye garden

Do you have a green thumb and do you want to raise your own environmentally green dyes? It's easy to grow your own. Rita Buchanan's book *A Dyer's Garden* (see the "Resource Guide" for details) is one of the most useful for North American gardeners. There are literally dozens of common plants that can be used for dyeing, from the yellow onion to Hopi red-dye amaranth, a beautiful addition to any garden and one that was traditionally used to dye ceremonial cornbread for Native American rituals. And since most dye plants are quite safe in the amounts used for dyeing, they're a fun experiment to try with children.

patterns

The patterns in this book, while written for specific yarns, are generally very accommodating of substitute yarns, provided they're of a similar weight. Many alt fiber yarns can pinch-hit for each other. For example, Habu Textiles' pineapple ramie blend and kenaf are almost exactly the same weight, but the pineapple is much more suitable for garments, while the kenaf is better for outerwear and accessories. When substituting yarns, be sure to knit a gauge swatch first and wash it to make sure the finished fabric is what you have in mind.

Starting off with sweaters, jackets, tops, and a sophisticated skirt, the pattern selection moves into wraps and scarves, socks, household items, and more. Unlike many wool or wool-blend yarns, alt fiber yarns are ideal for crisp, summery separates you can wear year-round, whether it's the two skirt/top/cardigan combos by Tamara Del Sonno or Nikol Lohr's fantastic linen skirt. There are socks aplenty, enough to satisfy even the most dedicated sock knitter, and accessories and home decor to surround yourself with these fabulous fibers.

linen-times-two skirt

BY NIKOL LOHR

This crisp little A-line skirt made from linen fiber and a linen stitch (linen-times-two!) is flattering to many shapes. The skirt closes at the top on both skirt hooks for smooth lines. You could substitute snap tape, Velcro, or hooks and eyes, if you prefer. The yarn comes in solids, or marled blends (different colored plies) for a tweedy look. The weighty linen stitch keeps the fabric from looking rumpled. We held a "scrunch test" with this skirt, and (amazingly, for linen) any wrinkles fell out almost immediately after letting go. This is a classic skirt you can wear for years.

SIZE

XS (S, M, L, 1X, 2X, 3X)

(It is shown here in size small.)

FINISHED MEASUREMENTS

Waist: 26 (28, 30, 32, 34, 36, 38)"

Length: 18 (18, 20, 20, 24, 24, 24)"

(Shorter and taller women can easily adjust length: measure from waist to where you want hemline, then follow pattern notes accordingly. Don't forget to get more yarn if you're lengthening.)

MATERIALS

Louet Euroflax (100% linen; 190 yd per 100 g skein); color: #43 Pewter; 5 (5, 6, 6, 7, 8) skeins

24" (or larger, for larger sizes) U.S. #7/4.5 mm circular needle, or size needed to obtain gauge (for body)

24" (or larger, for larger sizes) U.S. #4/3.5 mm circular needle, or size needed to obtain gauge (for hem and facing)

U.S. #4/E/3.5 mm crochet hook

Blunt yarn needle

Sharp embroidery needle

Stitch markers in 2 colors

6 sets of skirt hooks

GAUGE

20 sts and 40 rows = 4" in linen stitch, worked in the rnd, U.S. #7

PATTERN NOTES

Knit your swatch in the round on a 16" circular needle and use a 3-needle bind off to close the top. The reverse of linen stitch makes a dandy shower mitt (or washcloth, if you'd prefer to work your swatch flat). You'll be working these stitches both flat and round, so swatches of both would be a good idea. In either case, adjust for number of stitches by always staggering slipped and regular stitches. So slip the knits and knit the slips (or slip the purls and purl the slips, if you're looking at the wrong side and working flat).

Main Pattern (MP) Stitch (linen stitch)

In the rnd: Rnd 1: *k1, sl 1 wyif, rep from * to end. Rnd 2: *sl 1 wyif, k1, rep from * to end.

Flat: RS: *k1, sl 1 wyif, rep from * to end. WS: *p1, sl 1 wyib, rep from * to end.

continued

*Contrast Pattern (CP) Stitch
(slipped-stitch ribbing)*

In the rnd: Rnd 1: *k1, sl 1 wyib, rep from * to end. Rnd 2: *sl 1 wyib, k1, rep from * to end.

Flat: RS: *k1, sl 1 wyib, rep from * to end. WS: *p1, sl 1 wyif, rep from * to end.

YARN NOTES

While beautiful and refined, linen is not the most fun yarn to knit. It has no elasticity, so you have to provide all of the tension, which means it's hard on your hands. And because the plant fibers lack the cling and stretch of animal fibers, when you weave in the ends, you'll want to use a sharp needle and pierce the yarn you're weaving through. Weaving in an inch or so, then doubling back and piercing through the same fibers will also help secure the ends. I like to leave a short, knotted tail at the end. It's not gorgeous, but it gives your yarn a little wiggle room to migrate without having the cut end pop its way through to the right side of your work.

Louet highly recommends washing and drying your swatch, and warns that gauge can change dramatically, but I found that with the very dense stitches used here, washing and drying didn't have much effect. Speaking of washing and drying, the good news is that this yarn is machine washable. In fact, washing really contributes to the drape and softness of the finished fabric, and the extra workout of a machine (still on gentle/cold, mind you; let's not go crazy) conditions your finished fabric nicely. Plus there's no blocking (though you may want to iron it for a really crisp appearance).

directions

HEMLINE

With U.S. #4 needle, CO 120 (125,130, 135,140,145,150) sts, PM to mark one side, CO 121 (126,131,136,141,146,151) sts, PM to mark other side—241 (251, 261, 271, 281, 291, 301, 311) sts.

Join in the rnd, being careful not to twist sts.

Work 9 rnds in CP.

Dec rnd: dec 1 st either side of each marker—237 (247, 257, 267, 277, 287, 297, 307) sts.

Work 7 rnds in CP.

Work dec rnd again—233 (243, 253, 263, 273, 283, 293, 303) sts.

Set up transition to main pattern: Work rnd in CP, placing markers 5 (5, 6, 7, 8, 8, 9, 10) sts before and after side stitch markers (you can remove original side markers). This marks placement for the contrasting stitch stripes running along either side.

BEGIN MAIN PATTERN

Work CP on the 10–20 sts between the markers and MP in the main body of the patt.

DECREASE SKIRT

Maintain this patt, working MP across the front and back of skirt and CP in stripe along each side, until total length = 14 (14, 16, 16, 16, 16, 16, 16)" (see "Note" below).

At the same time, dec 4 sts every 8th (8th, 8th, 8th, 10th, 10th, 10th) rnd. Place dec on the MP side of each of the contrasting st markers (i.e., just outside each side of the CP stripe along skirt sides). I used k2tog before the stripe and ssk after, but use whichever you like. They'll be partially obscured by the pattern and further hidden by the slipped-stitch edging definition later.

Note: If you're adjusting the length, use the number here that corresponds to the length specified in the sizing. In general, this is 6" less than the overall length for sizes XS–L and 8" less than overall length for sizes XL–3XL.

SKIRT FRONT

(Please read over entire section before beginning work.)

You'll work the yoke flat, one side at a time. First you'll work the front, including the side stripe sts. Then you'll pu extra sts inside the skirt along the stripes and work the back just like the front. The front and back flaps you create will overlap and close along the stripes.

Work across in patt including the CP stripe. Turn work. Sl first st. Then, using flat version of both patts, cont across to the second contrast marker on the other side, k the last st. From here, you'll work the front half flat, back and forth, always slipping the first and k the last sts, and maintaining your st patts (MP flanked with CP on either side) and decs as outlined earlier, until the flap totals 5 (5, 5, 5, 7, 7, 7, 7)" long.

Then work 1" in CP, and BO in *k1, k2tog, rep (so instead of k each st before you BO, alternate between k and k2tog, BO after each in the usual way).

SKIRT BACK

You'll pu sts inside either side of the side stiching of the front flap, then k the back just as you did the front. The result will be two nearly identical skirt yoke flaps (the back flap has 2 more sts on either side) that overlap where they split.

With RS front of skirt facing you, fold down the flap you just k and, looking at the left side of the flap, locate row just below the unknit row of sts waiting on your needles. Looking down into the skirt (flap folded down) and starting 2 sts before the left-hand stripe stitching, one row below where the skirt splits, pu 12 (12, 14, 16, 18, 18, 20, 22) sts. PM, and with RS of back facing, cont to work across back of skirt sts in patt. When you get to the end of the row, PM and pu 12 (12, 14, 16, 18, 18, 20, 22) sts on the inside of the other side stripe, just as you did at the beg of the row.

From here, work Back exactly as for Front.

finishing

DEFINE PATTERN WITH CROCHET SLIP STITCHES (OPTIONAL)

With RS facing and starting at bottom right edge of side stripe (just above where CP switches to MP), work 1 crochet sl st sideways through each of the border sts. The row of sts will look like a crisp additional row of slipped-stitch ribbing, sharpening the edge of the pattern and obscuring the decs. This is optional but will sharpen the line between the MP and CP.

Break yarn when you reach the CP waist stitching, then work back down the other side.

Note: You're always working through the sts by inserting your hook from MP side into the first column of CP sts, so you'll work up the left side of the skirt and down the right. (So if you're approaching it from the side perspective, facing the stripes instead of the front/back, you'll work up the left side of the stripe and down the right.)

YOKE LINING

With U.S. #4 circular needle, starting along inside of front yoke flap edge (where skirt splits), pu one st for every sl st along side of yoke, PM, pu each st along top edge, PM, and pu one st for every sl st along other side of yoke.

Next and all even rows: k to 2 sts before marker, k2tog, SM, ssk, k to 2 sts before next marker, rep dec, k to end.

All odd rows: knit. Work 1" and BO. Rep on other yoke flap.

HEM LINING

With U.S. #4 circular needle and WS facing, pu 1 st for every st along the inside CO edge. K all rnds until length is just under length of contrast st hem, then BO.

Weave in all ends using a sharp embroidery needle, splitting the yarn and doubling back. I prefer to leave a short, knotted tail on each end on the inside after securing it well, just to be sure it won't eventually work its way out. You'll be able to hide almost all of your tails (certainly all of the lining and yoke tails) inside the yoke and hem lining when you sew it down.

Wash (machine gentle or by hand), dry (tumble low or air), and press skirt; then sew down the yoke and hem linings. When you sew down the lining, maintain an even tension to prevent bunching and hide your yarn tails under the lining as you sew it down (do check and make sure each has been secured—it will be impossible to weave them in later without ripping out the lining seams).

Try on the skirt before sewing on skirt hooks. If necessary, you can make the flaps overlap a bit more or less. Sew three hook halves of the skirt hooks carefully to either side of the wrong sides of front flap, spaced evenly and just barely inside the edge.

Sew bars just inside their mates just inside the contrast stitching (or at suitable locations for your fit) on the RS of the back flap so that the yoke flaps overlap at contrast stitching.

rose kilim sweater

BY ANDI SMITH AND SHANNON OKEY

The natural beauty of hand-dyed cotton is enhanced by this deceptively simple cable pattern adapted from *Vogue Knitting Stitchionary—Volume 2: Cables* (Sixth&Spring Books, 2006). This versatile cardigan will immediately become a classic to be worn for any occasion, and it will give you an opportunity to practice your natural dyeing skills, as described on pages 13–19.

SIZE

S (M, L, XL, XXL)

(It is shown here in size large.)

FINISHED MEASUREMENTS

Chest: 32 (36, 40, 44, 48)"

Sleeve: 17 (17, 18, 18, 19)"

Length: 22 (22, 23, 23 24)"

MATERIALS

Lion Cotton (100% organic cotton;
   5 oz/140 g per 236 yd/212 m balls);
   color: #760 098 Natural (hand dyed
   with plants; see page 19); color 1
   (C1): 6 (6, 6, 7, 7) skeins, color 2 (C2):
   2 skeins, and color 3 (C3): 1 skein

36" U.S. #9/5.5 mm circular needle,
   or size needed to obtain gauge

4 stitch holders or waste yarn

Waste yarn for provisional cast on

Large-eyed, blunt needle

GAUGE

16 sts and 16 rows = 4"
   in stockinette stitch

YARN NOTES

Hand-dyed yarn may leak color the first few times you wash it—in other words, don't throw it in with a load of white towels! You don't need to worry about all the color coming out, but natural dyes are more susceptible to fading than chemical ones, so don't leave it sitting in the backseat of your car for days on end!

directions

BACK

With waste yarn, provisionally CO 64 (72, 80, 88, 96) sts.

With C1, work in rev St st for 11 (11, 12, 13, 13)", ending with a WS row.

SHAPE ARMHOLE

With RS facing, BO 3 (4, 5, 6, 7) sts at beg of next 2 rows—58 (64, 70, 76, 82) sts.

Continue in rev St st until back measures 21 (21, 22, 23, 23)", then, with RS facing, divide for the neck as follows:

Row 1: p36 (40, 44, 48, 52), turn.

Row 2: BO 14 (16, 18, 20, 22) sts, turn—22 (24, 26, 28, 30) sts.

Row 3: purl.

Row 4: BO 3 sts, turn—19 (21, 23, 25, 27) sts.

Left Front

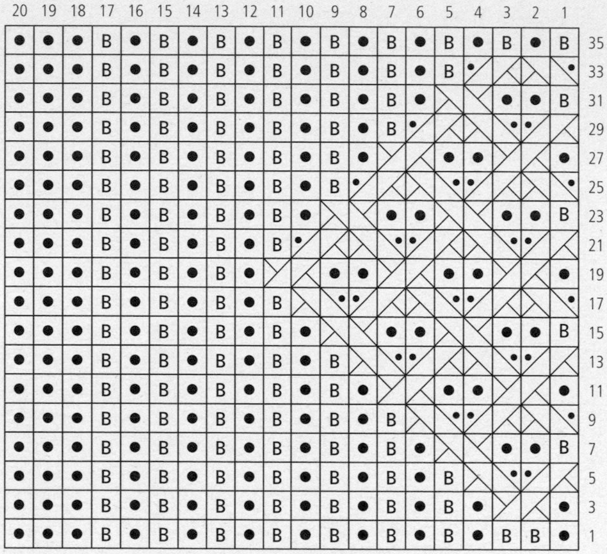
20 19 18 17 16 15 14 13 12 11 10 9 8 7 6 5 4 3 2 1
35 33 31 29 27 25 23 21 19 17 15 13 11 9 7 5 3 1

- Purl
- Knit tbl
- Right twist
- Right twist, purl background
- Left twist
- Left twist, purl background

Right Front

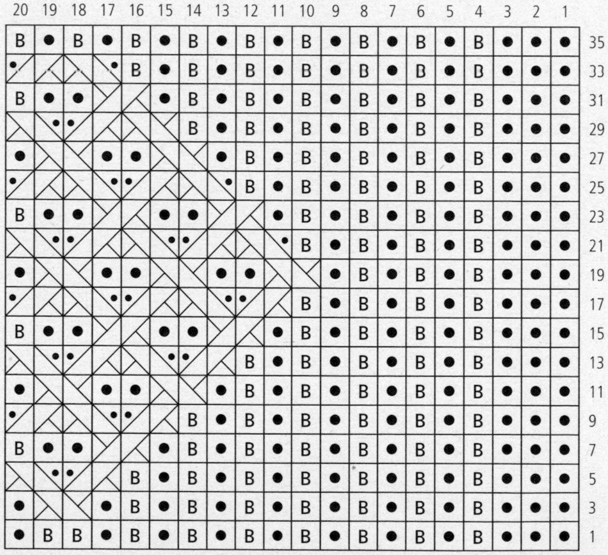
20 19 18 17 16 15 14 13 12 11 10 9 8 7 6 5 4 3 2 1
35 33 31 29 27 25 23 21 19 17 15 13 11 9 7 5 3 1

Row 5: p, then place sts onto st holder or waste yarn, leaving an 18" tail of yarn.

With RS facing,

Row 6: p rem 22 (24, 26, 28, 30) sts.

Row 7: knit.

Row 8: BO 3 sts—19 (21, 23, 25, 27) sts.

Row 9: knit.

Row 10: p, then place sts onto st holder or waste yarn, leaving an 18" tail of yarn.

LEFT FRONT

Using waste yarn, provisionally CO 32 (36, 40, 44, 48) sts.

Row 1 (RS): with C1, p13 (17, 21, 25, 29), *with C2, k1tbl, with C1, p1; rep from * 7 times, with C1, p2.

Row 2 (WS): with C1, k3, *with C2, p1, with C1, k1; rep from * 7 times, with C1, k to end.

Rep rows 1 and 2 for 3.5". Keeping continuity of colors as established, work the cable as set forth in the chart, then continue working rows 1 and 2 until work measures same length to armhole as back.

ARMHOLE

With RS facing, BO 3 (4, 5, 6, 7) sts, work in patt as established in Row 1 to end of row—29 (32, 35, 38, 41) sts.

Work 6 rows in patt, then BO 1 st at neck edge next and every following 4th row until 19 (21, 23, 25, 27) sts remain. Work in rem patt until front measures same

length as back. Place sts on st holder or waste yarn.

RIGHT FRONT

Using waste yarn, provisionally CO 32 (36, 40, 44, 48) sts.

Row 1 (RS): with C1, p3, *with C2, k1tbl, with C1, p1; rep from * 7 times, with C1, p to end.

Row 2 (WS): with C1, k13 (17, 21, 25, 29), *with C2, p1, with C1, k1, rep from * 7 times, with C1, p2.

Rep rows 1 and 2 for 3.5". Keeping continuity of colors as established, work the cable as set forth in the chart, then continue working rows 1 and 2 until work measures same length to armhole as back.

ARMHOLE

With WS facing, BO 3 (4, 5, 6, 7) sts, work in patt as established in Row 2 to end of row—29 (32, 35, 38, 41) sts.

Work 6 rows in patt, then BO 1 st at neck edge next and every following 4th row until 19 (21, 23, 25, 27) sts remain. Work in rem patt until front measures same length as left front and back. Place sts on st holder.

SLEEVES

With C3, CO 40 (40, 44, 44, 48) sts and work 6 rows in St st.

Row 7: with C1, p9 (9, 11, 11, 13) sts, *with C2, k1tbl, with C1, p1; rep from * 10 times, with C1, p to end.

Row 8: with C1, k9 (9, 11, 11, 13) sts, *with C2, p1, with C1, k1; rep from * 10 times, with C1, k to end.

Row 9: as Row 7.

Row 10: as Row 8.

Rep rows 7–10 inc 1 st at each end of next and then every foll 4th row until 78 (78, 82, 82, 86) sts rem, then work in patt as established until sleeve measures 17 (17, 18, 18, 19)" or desired length.

BO loosely.

finishing

Place sts from left front and left side of back onto needles and with WS tog, use Kitchener stitch to bind them tog. Rep the process for the right front. Attach sleeves, then sew side seams.

BOTTOM WELT

With bottom of left front facing, pu sts from provisional CO across the left front, then back, then right front.

With C3, work 6 rows of St st, then BO loosely.

FRONT WELT

With left front facing, using C3, pu 1 st for every 2 rows starting at bottom welt, up neck edge of left front, across the back and down the neck edge, and then across bottom welt of right front. Work 6 rows of St st, then BO loosely.

Weave in all ends and block.

audrey swing coat

BY TAMARA DEL SONNO

This is an Audrey Hepburn–inspired swing coat of fabulous proportion! It drapes in back and has jewelry-length sleeves—in jewel-tone colors—with wild little wiggles of bamboo feather. One big sparkly button holds the whole thing together.

SIZE

XS (S, M, L, 1X, 2X, 3X)

(It is shown here in size 1X.)

To fit bust: 28–30 (32–34, 36–38, 40–42, 44–46, 48–50, 52–54)"

FINISHED MEASUREMENTS

Chest: 34 (38, 42, 46, 50, 54, 58)"

Length: 18 (19, 20, 21, 22, 23, 24)" or desired length

MATERIALS

South West Trading Company Bamboo Feather (88% bamboo, 12% nylon; 110 yd per 50 g skein); color: #234 Black; 5 (5, 5, 6, 6, 7, 7) skeins

South West Trading Company Vickie Howell Collection CRAFT (65% organic cotton, 35% milk fiber; 125 m per 50 g skein); color: #767 Todd; 4 (4, 4, 5, 5, 6, 6) skeins

South West Trading Company Pure (100% SoySilk; 150 m per 50 g skein); color: #072 Blue Depths; 3 (3, 3, 4, 4, 5, 5) skeins

Buttons: 1 each Dill Company #330235/28 and #410028/Black

24" or 30" U.S. #13/9 mm circular needle, or size needed to obtain gauge

Extra #13 needle for 3-needle bind off

Removable stitch markers

3 stitch holders

Tapestry or yarn needle

GAUGE

9 sts and 12 rows = 4" in stockinette stitch, holding all 3 yarns together

PATTERN NOTES

Hold all three yarns together throughout project. The Bamboo Feather "feathers" throughout the coat create themselves; just don't hold the yarn too tightly while knitting.

Double Decrease

Slip 2 stitches together to the right needle, knit next stitch, slip passed stitches over knitted stitch to decrease, center decrease stitch over top of 2 decreases.

1 x 1 Rib

Knit 1 stitch, purl 1 stitch across row.

directions

BACK

CO 49 (57, 65, 73, 79, 87, 97) sts.

Work 4 rows of 1 x 1 ribbing, ending with k1.

Begin St st. Mark center st.

Row 1: k to 1 st before center, double decrease, k to end of row.

Rows 2 and 4: p all sts.

Row 3: k all sts.

Rep rows 1–4 to 15 (16, 18, 19, 20, 21, 22)" or desired length to underarm. At the same time, dec 1 st at each edge every 8 (8, 10, 10, 12, 12, 12) rows.

UNDERARM

BO 1 (1, 2, 2, 3, 3, 4) sts at beg of next 2 rows.

Work even in St st to 7 (7, 8, 9, 9, 10, 11)", dec at center as necessary to have 29 (31, 31, 33, 33, 35, 37) rem sts.

Work across 11 (12, 11, 12, 11, 12, 13) sts, dec 1 st, work to end of row.

Work 2 rows. Place rem sts on holder. Break yarn.

Place center 7 (7, 9, 9, 9, 11, 11) sts on holder for neck edge. Attach yarn, work to end of row.

Work toward neck edge, dec 1 st at neck edge. Work 2 rows. Place rem sts on holder. Break yarn.

LEFT FRONT

CO 25 (29, 33, 37, 39, 43, 49) sts

Work 4 rows of 1 x 1 ribbing.

Begin St st.

SHORT ROWS (SIDE EDGE)

Knit 8 (10, 11, 12, 13, 14, 16) sts, wrap and turn, p to end of row, k12 (15, 16, 18, 19, 21, 25) sts, wrap and turn, p to end of row, k16 (20, 22, 24, 26, 30, 34) sts, wrap and turn, p to end of row.

Work in St st, to match length at underarm to back at side seam. At the same time, dec every 4th row on side seam and every 8 (8, 10, 10, 12, 12, 12) rows at the center edge.

BO 1 (1, 2, 2, 3, 3, 4) sts at underarm edge, work to end of row.

Dec 1 st at neck edge every 4th row until 11 (12, 11, 12, 11, 12, 13) sts remain. Work even to match length of back armhole.

Place corresponding sts for the back shoulder on needle. Placing RS tog, work 3-needle bind off to attach left front shoulder to left back shoulder. Break yarn.

RIGHT FRONT

Rep Left Front, reversing shaping.

SLEEVES

With RS facing, start and end in corner of bound-off edge at underarm, pu and k3 sts for every 4 rows (approx 48 to 56 sts). Work in St st to 10 (10, 11, 11, 11, 12,

13)" or desired length. Work 4 rows of 1 x 1 rib. BO loosely. To taper sleeves slightly, work even 6", then dec 1 st at both edges of sleeve every 8th row.

FRONT EDGES: LEFT FRONT BAND

With RS facing, along front edge from neck edge point to bottom front edge, pu and k2 sts for every 3 rows.

Work 5 rows of 1 x 1 rib. BO in pattern.

FRONT EDGES: RIGHT FRONT BAND

With RS facing, along front edge from bottom front edge to neck edge point, pu and k2 sts for every 3 rows.

Row 1: work buttonholes from top edge, while working in 1 x 1 rib, as follows: work 2 sts, BO 1 st, PM, work 9 sts in rib, BO 1 st, PM, work 9 sts in rib, BO 1 st, PM, work in ribbing to end of row.

Row 2: in 1 x 1 rib, work to m, yo, work to m, yo, work to m, yo, work to end of row.

Rows 3–5: work in 1 x 1 rib as established. BO in patt.

COLLAR

With RS facing, pu sts from front corner of Right Front, k across sts on holder at back neck edge, and pu sts along front edge of Left Front.

Work 1 row of 1 x 1 rib, in established patt.

Work ribbing 4–6" or to desired length. BO in patt.

finishing

Sew side seams. Tuck in ends. Attach buttons in desired location on front of jacket (smaller button on top of larger one).

avery jacket

BY LAURA CHAU

The beauty of hemp yarn lies in its strength and durability as well as its incredible drape! Avery is a jacket you'll reach for over and over—easy to wear and easy care. Just drop this garment in the washing machine; it will get softer each time you wash it. You can even put it in the dryer if you like. This shapely jacket features streamlined front hems, long-sleeved plackets, and a no-fuss mandarin collar. Since hemp fabric isn't very stretchy, the jacket is designed with about four inches of positive ease.

SIZE

XS (S, M, L, 1X, 2X, 3X)

(It is shown here in size small.)

To fit bust: 28 (32, 36, 40, 44, 48, 52)"

FINISHED MEASUREMENTS

Bust: 32 (36, 40, 44, 48, 52, 56)"

Length: approximately 30"

MATERIALS

Hemp for Knitting Allhemp6 (165 yd/
  150 m per 100 g skein); color: #023
  Brick; 9 (10, 11, 12, 13, 15, 17) skeins

Straight or 24" circular U.S. #5/3.75 mm
  needle, or size needed to obtain gauge
  (for body)

16" or 24" circular U.S. #5/3.75 mm needle,
  or size needed to obtain gauge (for collar)

Stitch marker

Yarn or tapestry needle

Strong sewing thread to match yarn color

Sewing needle

8 2-piece fasteners

GAUGE

22 sts and 32 rows = 4" in woven stitch

PATTERN NOTES

Woven Stitch

> Row 1 (RS): *k1, sl 1 pwise wyif *,
> rep from * to * to last st, k1.
>
> Row 2 (WS): purl.
>
> Row 3: *sl 1 pwise wyif, k1*, rep from
> * to * to last st, sl 1 pwise wyif.
>
> Row 4: purl.
>
> Rep these 4 rows for pattern.

SPECIAL ABBREVIATIONS

wyib: with yarn in back

wyif: with yarn in front

directions

BACK

With straight or 24" circular needles, CO
117 (127, 137, 143, 159, 165, 181) sts.

Work 6 rows in woven stitch.

Row 1 (RS): work 42 (47, 52, 54, 62, 63,
69) sts in woven stitch, PM, p1, k30 (30,
33, 33, 33, 37, 41) sts, p1, PM, work 42
(47, 52, 54, 62, 63, 69) sts in woven stitch.

Row 2 (WS): work in patt to st marker, sl
m, k1, p30 (30, 33, 33, 33, 37, 41) sts, k1,
sl m, work in patt to end.

Rep rows 1 and 2 twice, maintaining
woven patt on side sections and St st with
border purl columns between markers.

Next (dec) row (RS): work in patt to marker,
sl m, p1, ssk, k to 3 before next marker,
k2tog, p1, sl m, work in patt to end.

Rep dec row every 4 (4, 4, 6, 6, 6, 6) rows 8 (8, 8, 8, 8, 9, 11) times, maintaining woven patt at each edge and St st with purl column border between the markers.

Next (dec) row (RS): k1, k2tog, work in patt to last 3 sts, ssk, k1.

Rep dec row every 4 (4, 4, 6, 6, 6, 6) rows 17 (17, 17, 14, 16, 13, 13) times—67 (77, 87, 99, 111, 121, 133) sts.

Work even in patt until piece measures 12.5 (12.5, 13, 14.5, 16.5, 17, 17.5, 18)" from beginning, ending with a WS row.

WAISTBAND

Row 1 (RS): p to marker, sl m, p1, k to 1 st before next marker, p1, sl m, p to end of row.

Row 2 (WS): p to marker, sl m, k1, p to 1 st before next marker, k1, p to end.

Row 3 (RS): k to marker, sl m, p1, k to 1 st before next marker, p1, k to end.

Rep rows 2 and 3 for 2", ending with a WS row.

Rep rows 1 and 2 once.

Next row (RS): work in woven stitch to marker, sl m, p1, k to 1 st before next marker, p1, sl m, work in woven st to end.

Work 3 rows even in woven stitch and St st pattern.

Next (inc) row (RS): k1, m1, work in patt to last st, m1, k1.

Rep inc row every 4 (4, 4, 6, 6, 6, 6) rows 10 (11, 12, 11, 11, 11, 11) times—87 (99, 111, 121, 133, 143, 155) sts.

Work even until piece measures 6 (6.25, 6.75, 7.5, 8, 8.25, 8.5)" from p row at end of waistband, ending with a WS row.

SHAPE ARMHOLE

BO 5 sts at beg of next 2 (2, 4, 4, 4, 6, 6) rows.

Next (dec) row: k1, k2tog, work in patt to last 3 sts, ssk, k1.

Rep dec row every RS row 5 (9, 7, 9, 12, 10, 14) times—67 (71, 77, 83, 89, 93, 97) sts.

Work even in patt until work measures 6.25 (6.75, 7.25, 7.75, 8.25, 8.75, 8.75)" from armhole bind offs.

Purl 1 row on RS. Work 1" even on all sts in St st.

SHAPE NECK

Next row (RS): k19 (20, 22, 23, 25, 27, 28) sts, BO center 29 (31, 33, 37, 39, 39, 41) sts, k rem 19 (20, 22, 23, 25, 27, 28) sts.

LEFT SHOULDER

BO 6 (6, 7, 7, 8, 9, 9) sts at beg of next WS row.

Work 1 row even.

BO 6 (7, 7, 8, 8, 9, 9) sts at beg of next WS row.

Work 1 row even.

BO rem 7 (7, 8, 8, 9, 9, 10) sts.

RIGHT SHOULDER

Rejoin yarn to right shoulder with WS facing.

Work 1 row even.

BO 6 (6, 7, 7, 8, 9, 9) sts at beg of next RS row.

Work 1 row even.

BO 6 (7, 7, 8, 8, 9, 9) sts at beg of next RS row.

Work 1 row even.

BO rem 7 (7, 8, 8, 9, 9, 10) sts.

LEFT FRONT

With straight or 24" circular needles, CO 67 (71, 77, 79, 87, 91, 99) sts.

Row 1 (RS): work 51 (55, 61, 63, 71, 75, 83) sts in woven st, k8, PM, sl 1 pwise wyib, k7.

Row 2 (WS): purl.

Rep rows 1 and 2 twice more.

Row 7: work 43 (47, 53, 53, 61, 63, 69) sts in woven stitch, PM, p1, k to next marker, sl 1 pwise wyib, k7.

Row 8: purl.

Rep rows 7 and 8 once more.

Next (dec) row (RS): work in patt to marker, sl m, p1, ssk, k to next marker, sl m, sl 1 pwise wyib, k7.

Rep dec row every 4 (4, 4, 6, 6, 6, 6) rows 8 (8, 8, 8, 8, 9, 11) times, maintaining woven patt at edge and St st with p column border and sl st fold line at center front.

Next (dec) row (RS): k1, k2tog, work in patt to end.

Rep dec row every 4 (4, 4, 6, 6, 6, 6) rows 17 (17, 17, 14, 16, 13, 13) times—67 (77, 87, 99, 111, 121, 133) sts.

Work even in patt until piece measures 12.5 (12.5, 13, 14.5, 16.5, 17, 17.5, 18)" from beginning, ending with a WS row.

WAISTBAND

Row 1 (RS): p to marker, sl m, p1, k to next marker, sl m, sl 1 pwise wyib, k7.

Row 2 (WS): p to second marker, sl m, k1, p to end.

Row 3 (RS): k to first marker, sl m, p1, k to next marker, sl m, sl 1 pwise wyib, k7.

Rep rows 2 and 3 for 2", ending with a WS row.

Rep rows 1 and 2 once more.

Next row (RS): work in woven stitch to marker, sl m, p1, k to next marker, sl 1 pwise wyib, k7.

Work 3 rows even in woven stitch and St st pattern.

Next (inc) row (RS): k1, m1, work in patt to end.

Rep inc row every 4 (4, 4, 6, 6, 6, 6) rows 10 (11, 12, 11, 11, 11, 11) times—87 (99, 111, 121, 133, 143, 155) sts.

Work even until piece measures 6 (6.25, 6.75, 7.5, 8, 8.25, 8.5)" from p row at end of waistband, ending with a WS row.

Read ahead! Armhole and neck shaping are worked at the same time.

SHAPE ARMHOLE

BO 5 sts at beg of next 1 (1, 2, 2, 2, 3, 3) row(s).

Next (dec) row: k1, k2tog, work in patt to end.

Rep dec row every RS row 5 (9, 7, 9, 12, 10, 14) times—67 (71, 77, 83, 89, 93, 97) sts.

Work even in patt until work measures 6.25 (6.75, 7.25, 7.75, 8.25, 8.75, 8.75)" from armhole bind offs

Purl 1 row on RS. Work 1" even on all sts in St st.

At the same time . . .

SHAPE NECK

When armhole measures 5 (5, 5.5, 5.5, 6, 6.5, 6.5)", BO 18 (18, 19, 20, 21, 22, 23) sts at beg of next WS row.

Next (dec) row: work in patt to last 3 sts, ssk, k1.

Rep dec row every RS row 5 (5, 6, 6, 6, 6, 6) times—19 (20, 22, 23, 25, 27, 28) sts.

Continue to end of armhole shaping. Shape left shoulder as for back.

RIGHT FRONT

With straight or 24" circular needles, CO 67 (71, 77, 79, 87, 91, 99) sts.

Row 1 (RS): k7, PM, sl 1 pwise wyib, work 51 (55, 61, 63, 71, 75, 83) sts in woven stitch.

Row 2 (WS): purl.

Rep rows 1 and 2 twice more.

Row 7: k to marker, sl m, sl 1 pwise wyib, k15, p1, PM, work 43 (47, 53, 53, 61, 63, 69) sts in woven stitch.

Row 8: purl.

Rep rows 7 and 8 once more.

Next (dec) row (RS): work in patt to marker, sl m, sl 1 pwise wyib, k to 3 sts before next marker, k2tog, p1, work in patt to end.

Rep dec row every 4 (4, 4, 6, 6, 6, 6) rows 8 (8, 8, 8, 8, 9, 11) times, maintaining woven patt at edge and St st with p column border and sl st fold line at center front.

Next (dec) row (RS): work in patt to last 3 sts, ssk, k1.

Rep dec row every 4 (4, 4, 6, 6, 6, 6) rows 17 (17, 17, 14, 16, 13, 13) times—67 (77, 87, 99, 111, 121, 133) sts.

Work even in patt until piece measures 12.5 (12.5, 13, 14.5, 16.5, 17, 17.5, 18)" from beg, ending with a WS row.

WAISTBAND

Row 1 (RS): k to marker, sl m, sl 1 pwise wyib, k to 1 st before next marker, p1, p to end.

Row 2 (WS): p to marker, sl m, k1, p to end.

Row 3 (RS): k to marker, sl m, sl 1 pwise wyib, k to 1 st before marker, p1, k to end.

Rep rows 2 and 3 for 2", ending with a WS row.

Rep rows 1 and 2 once more.

Next row (RS): k to marker, sl m, sl 1 pwise wyib, k to 1 st before next marker, p1, work in woven stitch to end.

Work 3 rows even in woven stitch and St st pattern.

Next (inc) row (RS): work in patt to last st, m1, k1.

Rep inc row every 4 (4, 4, 6, 6, 6, 6) rows 10 (11, 12, 11, 11, 11, 11) times—87 (99, 111, 121, 133, 143, 155) sts.

Work even until piece measures 6 (6.25, 6.75, 7.5, 8, 8.25, 8.5)" from p row at end of waistband, ending with a RS row.

Read ahead! Armhole and neck shaping are worked at the same time.

SHAPE ARMHOLE

BO 5 sts at beg of next 1 (1, 2, 2, 2, 3, 3) row(s).

Next (dec) row: work in patt to last 3 sts, ssk, k1.

Rep dec row every RS row 5 (9, 7, 9, 12, 10, 14) times—67 (71, 77, 83, 89, 93, 97) sts.

Work even in patt until work measures 6.25 (6.75, 7.25, 7.75, 8.25, 8.75, 8.75)" from armhole bind offs.

Purl 1 row on RS. Work 1" even on all sts in St st.

At the same time . . .

SHAPE NECK

When armhole measures 5 (5, 5.5, 5.5, 6, 6.5, 6.5)", BO 18 (18, 19, 20, 21, 22, 23) sts at beg of next RS row.

Work 1 row even in patt.

Next (dec) row: work in patt to last 3 sts, ssk, k1.

Rep dec row every RS row 5 (5, 6, 6, 6, 6, 6) times—19 (20, 22, 23, 25, 27, 28) sts.

Continue to end of armhole shaping. Shape right shoulder as for back.

SLEEVES (MAKE TWO)

With straight or 24" circular needles, CO 65 (67, 69, 73, 75, 79, 81) sts.

Row 1 (RS): k5, PM, sl 1 pwise wyib, k6, PM, work 41 (43, 45, 49, 51, 55, 57) sts in woven stitch, PM, k6, PM, sl 1 pwise wyib, k5.

Row 2: purl.

Rep rows 1 and 2, slipping markers, until piece measures 6 (6, 6, 6, 7, 7, 7)" from beg, ending with a WS row.

Next row (RS): BO 6, work in woven stitch to end.

Next row (WS): BO 6, p to end.

Next (inc) row: k1, m1, work in woven stitch to last st, m1, k1.

Rep inc row every 6 (6, 6, 6, 4, 4, 4) rows · 11 (12, 14, 15, 17, 17, 19) times total.

Work even until sleeve measures 18 (18.5, 19, 19, 19.5, 19.5, 20)" from beg.

BO 5 sts at beg of next 2 (2, 4, 4, 4, 6, 6) rows.

Next (dec) row (RS): k1, k2tog, work in patt to last 3 sts, ssk, k1.

Rep dec row every RS row 16 (18, 18, 20, 22, 22, 24) times.

BO 3 sts at beg of next 4 (4, 4, 4, 6, 6, 2) rows.

BO 2 sts at beg of next 2 (2, 0, 2, 2, 2, 2) rows

BO rem 17 (17, 17, 17, 19, 19, 19) sts.

finishing

Weave in ends on all pieces. Machine wash in warm water. Tumble dry until damp, remove, and let air-dry, or remove pieces from washing machine and let air-dry.

With sewing thread held doubled or quadrupled, use mattress stitch to sew the seams in the order shown below. On the WS of the fabric, pu the horizontal bar in the st next to the edge, then the corresponding bar st on the other piece, and cont as established, weaving your thread

back and forth horizontally. Pull the thread taut (but not too tight) to close up the seam opening. Mattress stitch should be nearly invisible on the piece's RS.

Sew shoulder seams.

Sew side seams.

Sew hems on sleeves and body, folding vertically along slipped stitch.

Sew sleeve seams.

Set in sleeves.

COLLAR

With 16" or 24" circular needle, join yarn with RS facing at right front edge and pu and k sts around neck for collar as follows:

8 sts along right front band, 1 st in every other row along right front neck, 1 st in each st along back neck, 1 st in every other row along left front neck, 8 sts along left front band.

Row 1 (WS): purl.

Row 2 (RS): sl 3 sts pwise wyib, k to last 3 sts, sl 3 sts pwise wyib.

Rep rows 1 and 2, 4 times total, then rep Row 1 once (9 rows worked in total).

Next row (RS): sl 3 sts pwise wyib, ssk, k to last 6 sts, k3tog, sl 3 sts pwise wyib.

Next row (WS): p3, p3tog, p to last 6 sts, p3tog tbl, p3.

Next row (RS): p all sts.

Work 10 rows in St st. BO all sts.

Weave in ends and machine wash once more.

Fold collar facing to inside along p row. Sew to first row of collar with sewing thread.

Sew on fasteners as follows:

Sew 2 on each sleeve placket, at 2.5" and 4.5" from bottom.

Sew 4 along front with highest at the base of the collar, the lowest in the middle of the waistband, and the other 2 evenly spaced between.

fern tee

BY KATE JACKSON

At last—a knitted top as comfortable as your most worn-out T-shirt (you know the one)! With its lovely lacy details on top, this is something you can wear for work and play. The corn fiber fabric is astonishingly soft, and comfortable even on the hottest days. Just don't iron it (corn fiber melts at high heat). Besides, who wants to iron her favorite top?

SIZE

S (M, L)

(It is shown here in size small.)

FINISHED MEASUREMENTS

Chest: 32 (35, 38)"

Length: 19 (20, 21)"

MATERIALS

South West Trading Company aMAIZing (100% corn fiber; 130 m per 50 g skein); color: 367 Clove; 5 (6, 7) balls

24" U.S. #7/4.5 mm circular needle, or size needed to obtain gauge (for body)

16" U.S. #7 circular needle, or size needed to obtain gauge (for neckline and sleeves)

GAUGE

20 sts and 26 rows – 4" in stockinette stitch

directions

BACK

With 24" needle, provisionally CO 23 (27, 27) sts for the right shoulder.

Row 1: purl.

Row 2: k12, wrap and turn, p12, k3 (5, 5), (yo, k2, ssk, k2tog, k2, yo, k1) twice, k2 (4, 4).

Row 3: purl.

Break yarn and set aside.

Provisionally CO 23 (27, 27) sts for left shoulder.

Row 1: p12, wrap and turn, k12, p to end, working wrapped st tog with the wrap.

Row 2: k2 (4, 4), (yo, k2, ssk, k2tog, k2, yo, k1) twice, k3 (5, 5).

Row 3: purl.

Row 4: k3 (5, 5), (yo, k2, ssk, k2tog, k2, yo, k1) twice, k2 (4, 4), CO 23 (18, 27),

then work right shoulder sts from holder as follows k2 (4, 4), (yo, k2, ssk, k2tog, k2, yo, k1) twice, k3 (5, 5)—69 (72, 81) sts.

Rows 5 and 7: purl.

Row 6: k4 (5, 5), (yo, k2, ssk, k2tog, k2, yo, k1) to last sts, k2 (4, 4).

Row 8: k3 (4, 4), (yo, k2, ssk, k2tog, k2, yo, k1) to last sts, k3 (5, 5).

Rep the last 4 rows for patt, until piece measures 6" from center back neck.

Change to St st and work even for 2 rows.

Next 3 (4, 4) RS rows: k2, m1 left leaning, k to last 2 sts, m1 right leaning, k2—75 (80, 89) sts.

P 1 row. Place sts on a holder and set aside.

LEFT FRONT SHOULDER

Pu 23 (27, 27) sts from provisional CO of left shoulder.

Row 1: purl.

Row 2: k10, wrap and turn, p10.

Row 3: k2 (4, 4), (yo, k2, ssk, k2tog, k2, yo, k1) twice, k3 (5, 5).

Row 4: purl.

Row 5: k3 (5, 5), (yo, k2, ssk, k2tog, k2, yo, k1) twice, k2 (4, 4).

Row 6: purl.

Rep the last 4 rows until there are 8 fewer rows than was done for the lace. Inc 1 st at neck edge on next 4 RS rows as follows: k1, m1 left leaning, work in patt to end. The new sts should be worked in St st after they are made—27 (31, 31) sts.

P 1 row, place on holder, and set aside.

RIGHT FRONT SHOULDER

Pu 23 (27, 27) sts from provisional CO of right shoulder.

Row 1: p10, wrap and turn, k10.

Row 2: purl.

Row 3: k2 (4, 4), (yo, k2, ssk, k2tog, k2, yo, k1) twice, k3 (5, 5).

Row 4: purl.

Row 5: k3 (5, 5), (yo, k2, ssk, k2tog, k2, yo, k1) twice, k2 (4, 4).

Row 6: purl.

Rep the last 4 rows as for left shoulder. Inc 1 st at neck edge on next 4 RS rows as follows: Work in patt to last st, m1 right leaning, k1. The new sts should be worked in St st after they are made—27 (31, 31) sts.

P 1 row. You are now completely done with the lace pattern, and the rest of the tee is done in St st.

FRONT

Row 1: k27 (31, 31) sts of right shoulder, CO 15 (10, 19) sts, and k27 (31, 31) sts of left shoulder from holder—69 (72, 81) sts.

Rows 2, 4, and 6: purl.

Rows 3, 5, and 7: k2, m1 left leaning, k to last 2 sts, m1 right leaning, k2.

Row 8: purl—75 (80, 89) sts.

BODY

Joining rnd: k75 (80, 89) front sts, PM to designate halfway point, k75 (80, 89) sts from back holder, PM for bind-off row—150 (160, 178) sts.

K every rnd until tee measures 6" from end of lace patt.

Dec rnd: (k2, ssk, k to 4 sts from marker, k2tog, k2) twice.

Work even for 1", then rep dec rnd—142 (152, 170) sts.

Work even until tee measures 9" from end of lace panel.

Inc rnd: (k2, m1 left leaning, k to 2 sts from marker, m1 right leaning, k2) twice.

Work even for 1", then rep inc rnd—150 (160, 178) sts.

Work even until tee measures 13.5 (15, 16.5)" from end of lace panel and 19.5 (21, 22.5)" from center back neck.

NECK EDGING

With 16" needle, pu and k100 (110, 120) sts around neckline. P 2 rnds. BO pwise.

SLEEVES

With 16" needle, beg at the center bottom of the sleeve opening, pu and k72 (76, 76) sts around opening.

Row 1: k42 (44, 44), wrap and turn.

Row 2: p12, wrap and turn.

Row 3: k12, k next st with its wrap, wrap and turn.

Row 4: p13, p next st with its wrap, wrap and turn.

Cont, working 1 more st each row.

The last short row will be: k40 (42, 44), k next st with its wrap, DO NOT TURN, k to marker.

Note: You can adjust this next dec rnd to customize the fit of the sleeve to the width of your upper arm.

Dec rnd: k1, k2tog, (k2, k2tog) twice, k12, k2tog, k to last 25 sts, ssk, k12 (ssk, k2) twice, ssk, k1—64 (68, 68) sts.

P 1 rnd. BO pwise.

finishing

Weave in ends and block.

bow tank

BY JENNY WILLEY

This versatile tank is simple to knit and fun to wear. In a bright color, as shown on page 44, it's fresh and young. Knit it in neutrals or one solid color for a more sophisticated look. (Black and white would look quite mod!)

SIZE

XS (S, M, L, 1X, 2X, 3X)

(It is shown here in size small.)

To fit bust: 28–30 (32–34, 36–38, 40–42, 44–46, 48–50, 52–54)"

FINISHED MEASUREMENTS

Chest: 32 (36, 40, 44, 48, 52, 56)"

Length: 14 (15, 15, 16, 16, 17, 17)"

MATERIALS

South West Trading Company Vickie Howell Collection LOVE (70% bamboo, 30% silk; 90 m per 50 g skein); main color (MC): Clarence & Alabama, 5 (6, 6, 7, 8, 9, 10) skeins; contrasting color (CC): June & Johnny, 2 (2, 2, 2, 3, 3, 3) skeins

24" or 29" U.S. #7/4.5 mm circular needle, or size needed to obtain gauge

24" or 29" U.S. #9/5.5 mm circular needle, or size needed to obtain gauge

Tapestry needle

Stitch marker

GAUGE

20 sts and 28 rows = 4" in stockinette stitch, U.S. #7

20 sts and 32 rows = 4" in linen stitch, U.S. #9

PATTERN NOTES

Linen Stitch Body

Knit in the round with an odd number of stitches: knit 1, *sl 1, wyif, knit 1*. Rep from * to *.

Straps

Knit flat with an odd number of stitches:

Row 1: k1, *sl 1, wyif, k1*. Rep from * to *.

Row 2: k1, p1, *sl 1, wyib, p1*, k1. Rep from * to *.

SPECIAL ABBREVIATIONS

wyib: with yarn in back

wyif: with yarn in front

directions

Using #9 needle and MC, CO 161 (181, 201, 221, 241, 261, 281) sts. Join in the rnd, taking care not to twist. Work 4" in linen stitch.

Change to #7 needle, work 8 (9, 9, 10, 10, 11, 11)" of St st.

Change back to #9 needle, work 3 (3, 3.5, 3.5, 4, 4, 4.5)" of linen stitch.

EYELET ROW FOR RIBBON SASH

Work 9 (11, 10, 11, 11, 12, 13) sts, k2tog, yo, yo, k2tog, work 9 (11, 10, 12, 11, 12, 14) sts, k2tog, yo, yo, k2tog. Rep from * to * around, k5 (1, 5, 4, 1, 5, 1) sts—12 (12, 14, 14, 16, 16, 16) eyelets created.

K 1 rnd, working k1, p1 into each yo, yo.

Work 0.5" of linen stitch. BO.

RIBBON

Using CC and #7 needle, CO 8 sts. Work 1 x 1 ribbing for 30 (34, 38, 42, 46, 50, 54)".

Do not BO.

Thread ribbon through eyelets.

BOWTIE

**Maintaining 1 x 1 ribbing patt, yo at beg of every row to 24 (24, 24, 26, 26, 28, 28) sts per row. K2tog beg of every row to 12 (12, 12, 12, 14, 14, 14) sts, continue in patt 6"–10" for tie end of bow. BO in patt.

Pu 8 sts at CO edge and rep from **.

That's it! You're done.

bamboo cardigan trio

BY TAMARA DEL SONNO

This cardigan set features a V-neck tank and an elastic-waisted skirt with fabulous—but optional—flares around the skirt and cardigan bottom. Each item works great in the set or stands on its own as a fashion basic.

SIZE

XS (S, M, L, 1X, 2X, 3X)

(It is shown here in size large.)

To fit bust measurement: 28–30 (32–34, 36–38, 40–42, 44–46, 48–50, 52–54)"

FINISHED MEASUREMENTS

Tank

Chest: 30 (34, 38, 42, 46, 50, 54)"

Length: 16 (17, 18, 18, 19, 20, 20)" or desired length

Cardigan

Chest: 34 (38, 42, 46, 50, 54, 58)"

Skirt

Hip: 30 (34, 38, 42, 46, 50, 54)"

Length: 20 (22, 24, 25, 26, 27, 28)" or desired length

MATERIALS

Universal Yarn Inc., Panda (100% bamboo; 98 yd per 50 g skein); color: #8

Stitch holders

Removable stitch markers

Tapestry needle

Note: Smaller sizes use the shorter circular needle and larger sizes use the longer circular needle in the following needle-length recommendations.

Tank 6 (7, 8, 9, 10, 11, 12) skeins

24"–30" U.S. #6/4 mm circular needle

24"–30" U.S. #7/4.5 mm circular needle

Cardigan: 9 (9, 10, 11, 12, 13, 14) skeins

24"–30" U.S. #8/5 mm circular needle

24"–30" U.S. #9/5.5 mm circular needle

24"–30" U.S. #10/6 mm circular needle

Skirt: 7 (7, 8, 9, 10, 11, 11) skeins

24"–30" U.S. #7/4.5 mm circular needle

24"–30" U.S. #8/5 mm circular needle

24"–30" U.S. #9/5.5 mm circular needle

24"–30" U.S. #10/6 mm circular needle

1"-wide nonroll elastic, desired length around waist, for waistband

Sewing needle

Coordinating thread

GAUGE

Tank: 22 sts and 26 rows = 4" in stockinette stitch, U.S. #7

Cardigan: 18 sts and 21 rows = 4" in stockinette stitch, U.S. #10

Skirt: 20 sts and 24 rows = 4" in stockinette stitch, U.S. #9

PATTERN NOTES

Double Decrease

Slip 2 stitches together to the right needle, knit next stitch, slip passed stitches over knitted stitch to decrease, center decrease stitch over top of 2 decreases.

tank directions

BACK

Using #6 needle and knit on method, CO: 82 (94, 104, 116, 126, 136, 148) sts.

Work 1" in St st.

Change to #7 needle, p 1 row on RS.

In St st, work 8 (9, 9, 10, 11, 12, 13)" or length desired to underarm.

FINISH BACK

BO 2 (3, 3, 4, 5, 5, 6) sts at beg of next 2 rows.

Dec 1 st at both edges, every other row 2 (2, 3, 4, 5, 5, 6) times.

Work to 6 (6.5 7, 7.5, 8, 8.5 9)" from beg or 1" less than desired depth of armhole.

WORK SHOULDERS

Work 24 (27, 29, 32, 35, 38, 41) sts, turn, dec 1 st, work to end of row.

Work 1 row even. Dec at neck edge of next row.

Cont in St st for 6 rows. Place sts on holder. Break yarn—22 (25, 27, 30, 33, 36, 39) sts.

Place center 24 (26, 30, 32, 36, 42) sts on holder for neck edge. Attach yarn at neck edge of rem back shoulder sts, dec 1 st, work to end of row.

Work 1 row even. Dec at neck edge of next row. Cont in St st for 6 rows. Place sts on holder. Break yarn—20 (23, 25, 38, 31, 34, 37) sts.

FRONT

Work as for Back to 1"–1.5" before desired length to underarm, then begin shaping.

SHAPE FRONT (OPTIONAL)

Choose shaping based on bra-cup size as follows:

A-cup: work to 5 sts before side, wrap and turn, work to 5 sts before opposite side, wrap and turn, work to end of row.

Go to underarm and neckline.

B-cup: work to 5 sts before side, wrap and turn, work to 5 sts before opposite side, wrap and turn, work to end of row. Work 1 row. Work to 10 sts before side, wrap and turn, work to 10 sts before opposite side, wrap and turn, work to end of row.

Go to underarm and neckline.

C-cup: work to 5 sts before side, wrap and turn, work to 5 sts before opposite side, wrap and turn, work to end of row. Work 1 row. Work to 8 sts before side, wrap and turn, work to 8 sts before opposite side, wrap and turn, work to end of row. Work 1 row. Work to 12 sts before side, wrap and turn, work to 12 sts before opposite side, wrap and turn, work to end of row.

Go to underarm and neckline.

D-cup: work to 5 sts before side, wrap and turn, work to 5 sts before opposite side, wrap and turn, work to end of row. Work 1 row. Work to 8 sts before side, wrap and turn, work to 8 sts before opposite side, wrap and turn, work to end of row. Work 1 row. Work to 12 sts before side, wrap and turn, work to 12 sts before opposite

side, wrap and turn, work to end of row. Work to 18 sts before side, wrap and turn, work to 18 sts before opposite side, wrap and turn, work to end of row.

Go to underarm and neckline.

UNDERARM AND NECKLINE

BO 2 (3, 3, 4, 5, 5, 6) sts beg next 2 rows. Dec 1 st at both edges, every other row 2 (2, 3, 4, 5, 5, 6) times.

At the same time: divide into 2 sections, put center 2 sts on holder. Work sides separately.

Dec 1 st at neck edge every other row until 20 (23, 25, 38, 31, 34, 37) sts remain. Work to match length of Back. Place sts on holder. Rep on second side.

finishing

Join shoulder seams tog by matching corresponding sts on needles, work 3-needle bind off.

CREATE HEM EDGING FOR ARMHOLES

Using #7 needle, with RS facing, begin at center underarm.

Pu sts around armhole, approx 2 sts per 3 rows. Work 1" St st, p 1 row on the RS.

Change to #6 needle, work 1" St st.

BO: *k2tog, put newly made st from right needle back onto left needle,* rep from * to * around. Break yarn. Fold over at p row and sew bound-off edge inside for hem.

Rep for second arm, closely matching number of sts.

CREATE HEM EDGING FOR NECKLINE

Using #7 needle, with RS facing, begin at center shoulder seam.

Pu sts along neckline, approx 2 sts per 3 rows. K the centerpoint marked sts tog and retain marker at center neck, pu sts along back edge, k sts off holder, pu sts along second side to join in rnd. Mark beg.

Work 1" St st; p 1 round on the RS.

At the same time: double decrease over st marked at center front of neck, every other row.

Change to #6 needle, work 1" St st. DO NOT dec at center marked st.

BO: *k2tog, put newly made st from right needle back onto left needle,* rep from * to * around. Break yarn. Fold over at p row and sew bound-off edge inside for hem.

Join side seams.

Bottom: turn up hem at p row; sew into place.

cardigan directions

BACK

Using #9 needle, CO 22 (22, 22, 24, 24, 25, 27) sts. Work 1" St st. Place sts on holder—CO 22 (22, 22, 24, 24, 25, 27) sts.

Work 1" St st. Using the knit on method, CO 19 (21, 23, 24, 26, 26, 27) sts between the pair of shoulder sts, join and work across sts on holder—63 (65, 67, 72, 74, 76, 81) sts.

Work in St st for 6 (7, 8, 8.5, 9, 10, 11)" or desired depth to underarm. CO 2 (3, 4, 4, 5, 6, 6) sts at the beg of the next 2 rows—67 (71, 75, 80, 84, 88, 93) sts.

Work in St st for 6 (7, 8, 9, 10, 11, 12)" or desired length to top of flares.

BO: *k2tog, put newly made st from right needle back onto left needle,* rep from * to * around.

LEFT FRONT

Using #9 needle, CO 22 (22, 22, 24, 24, 25, 27) sts. Work 2" St st. Inc 1 st at neck edge every 4th row to desired length at underam or to 35 (36, 38, 41, 42, 44, 46) sts and work even to 6 (7, 8, 8.5, 9, 10, 11)" or desired length to underarm.

Knit on 2 (3, 4, 4, 5, 6, 6) sts at the beg of the underarm side and if necessary cont inc sts at front corner of cardigan. Work even in St st to length of Back to start top of flares—37 (39, 42, 45, 47, 50, 52) sts.

BO: *k2tog, put newly made st from right needle back onto left needle,* rep from * to * around. Do not break yarn.

RIGHT FRONT

Work as for Left Front, reversing shaping. Break yarn after BO.

SLEEVES

Sew shoulder seams together.

Using #9 needle, with RS facing, pu sts using following formula: *3 sts for every 4 rows, then 2 sts for every 3 rows*, rep from * to * from corner of underarm up along shoulder, down to second corner, do not pu along flat of underarm to seam.

Pu approx 56 (66, 76, 80, 86, 96, 100) sts per sleeve.

Work St st even for 3". Dec 1 st at beg and end of every 6th row. Work to 14"–17" or desired length before flares.

BO: *k2tog, put newly made st from right needle back onto left needle,* rep from * to * around. Do not break yarn.

SLEEVE FLARE RUFFLE

Using #10 needle, pu 54 (66, 76, 80, 86, 96, 100) sts along bound-off edge.

Row 1: k7 (9, 10, 12, 13, 14, 14), m1 right leaning, k1 (mark as inc st), m1 left leaning, k7 (9, 11, 11, 12, 14, 15), double decrease, k7 (9, 11, 11, 12, 14, 15), m1 right leaning, k1 (mark st), m1 left leaning, k7 (9, 11, 11, 12, 14, 15), double decrease, k7 (9, 11, 11, 12, 14, 15), m1 right leaning, k1 (mark st), m1 left leaning, k7 (9, 10, 12, 13, 14, 14), double decrease.

Row 2: purl.

Row 3: k1, m1 right leaning, k1, m1 left leaning at the marked inc sts from Row 1.

Row 4: purl.

Row 5: k9 (11, 12, 14, 15, 16, 16), m1 right leaning, k1, m1 left leaning, k8 (10,

12, 13, 13, 15, 16), k3tog, k8 (10, 12, 12, 13, 15, 16), m1 right leaning, k1, m1 left leaning, k8 (10, 12, 12, 13, 15, 16), k3tog, k8 (10, 12, 12, 13, 15, 16), m1 right leaning, k1, m1 left leaning, k8 (10, 11, 13, 14, 15, 15), k3tog.

Row 6: purl.

Work rows 1–6, twice. Inc before and after the marked st; the st count will cont to change as the flare grows.

Work rows 3 and 4, 3 times.

Knit 1 row on the WS. Work 1" St st.

BO loosely.

Sew seam from flare to underarm of sleeve.

Fold hem up to WS at p row and sew into place.

BOTTOM FLARE

Sew seams from bottom of cardigan up to underarm.

Using #10 needle, pu sts from the RS, along bound-off edge, place markers at side seams.

There are 2 peaks on each front and 3 on the back.

Row 1: k9 (9, 10, 10, 10, 12, 12), m1 right leaning, k1 (mark st), m1 left leaning, k7 (9, 9, 10, 11, 11, 12), double decrease, k7 (9, 9, 10, 11, 11, 12), m1 right leaning, k1 (mark st), m1 left leaning, k9 (9, 9, 10, 10, 11, 11). (PM between front and side.) K9 (11, 11, 11, 11, 13, 14), m1 right leaning, k1 (mark st), m1 left leaning, k10 (10, 11, 12, 13, 13, 14), double decrease, k10 (10,

11, 12, 13, 13, 14), m1 right leaning, k1 (mark st), m1 left leaning, k10 (10, 11, 12, 13, 13, 14), double decrease, k10 (10, 11, 12, 13, 13, 14), m1 right leaning, k1 (mark st), m1 left leaning, k9 (11, 11, 12, 12, 14, 14), double decrease. (PM between front and side.) K9 (9, 9, 10, 10, 11, 11), m1 right leaning, k1 (mark st), m1 left leaning, k7 (9, 9, 10, 11, 11, 12), double decrease, k7 (9, 9, 10, 11, 11, 12), m1 right leaning, k1 (mark st), m1 left leaning, k9 (9, 10, 10, 11, 12, 12)—7 inc sts marked; markers at 2 side seams.

Row 2: knit.

Row 3: k, inc before and after 7 marked inc sts from Row 1 by: m1 right leaning, k1, m1 left leaning.

Row 4: knit.

Row 5: k11 (11, 12, 12, 12, 13, 13), m1 right leaning, k1, m1 left leaning, k8 (10, 10, 11, 12, 12, 13), k3tog, k8 (10, 10, 11, 12, 12, 13), m1 right leaning, k1, m1 left leaning, k11 (11, 12, 12, 12, 13, 13). (PM between front and side.) K11 (13, 13, 13, 13, 15, 16), m1 right leaning, k1, m1 left leaning, k11 (11, 12, 13, 14, 14, 15), k3tog, k11 (11, 12, 13, 14, 14, 15), m1 right leaning, k1, m1 left leaning, k11 (11, 12, 13, 14, 14, 15), k3tog, k11 (11, 12, 13, 14, 14, 15), m1 right leaning, k1, m1 left leaning, k10 (12, 12, 14, 14, 16, 16). (PM between front and side.) K11 (11, 12, 12, 12, 13, 13), m1 right leaning, k1, m1 left leaning, k8 (10, 10, 11, 12, 12, 13), k3tog, k8 (10, 10, 11, 12, 12, 13), m1 right leaning, k1, m1 left leaning, k11 (11, 12, 12, 12, 13, 13).

Work rows 1–6, twice. Inc before and after the marked st; the st count will cont to change as the flare grows.

Work rows 3 and 4, 3 times.

K 1 row on the WS. Work 1" St st.

BO loosely.

Sew seam from flare to underarm of sleeve.

Fold hem up to WS at p row and sew into place.

finishing

FRONT EDGES AND NECKLINE

Using #9 needle, with RS facing, pu sts using following formula: *3 sts for every 4 rows, then 2 sts for every 3 rows* alternate these two choices up one front, mark corner front, work up neckline, k up holder across back neckline, down the second side. Work 1" St st, work m1 inc on RS rows at corner points.

Work 1 row p on the RS. Change to #8 needle and work 1" and 1 row of St st.

BO: *k2tog, put newly made st from right needle back onto left needle,* rep from * to * around. Fold over hem and stitch down.

skirt directions

Using #7 needle and knit on method, CO 142 (162, 182, 202, 222, 242, 262) sts.

Join, being careful not to twist, PM at beg of rnd and k 1.25" in the rnd.

Change to #8 needle, p 1 rnd, then k 1.5".

PM at halfway point to identify sides for shaping.

K1, m1, k to 1 before 2nd (new) marker, m1, k2, m1 left leaning, k to 1 before end of rnd marker, m1 left leaning, k1—146 (166, 186, 206, 226, 246, 266) sts.

K4 (4, 5, 5, 6, 6, 7) rnds even.

K1, m1 left leaning, k to 1 before marker, m1 left leaning, k2, m1 left leaning, k to 1 before end of rnd marker, m1 left leaning, k1.

K4 (4, 5, 5, 6, 6, 7) rnds—150 (170, 190, 210, 230, 250, 270) sts.

Inc rnd: k1, m1 left leaning, *k14 (16, 18, 20, 22, 24, 26) sts, m1 left leaning*, rep from * to *, k9, m1 left leaning—162 (182, 202, 222, 242, 262, 282) sts.

Work in St st 12"–16" or desired length to ruffle (ruffle is approx 5" long).

Note: skirt will hang longer than it appears as knit because of weight of ruffle when completed.

BO: *k2tog, put newly made st from right needle back onto left needle,* rep from * to * around. Do not break yarn.

FLARE RUFFLE

Working in the rnd and using #10 needle, pu sts along bound-off edge, one to one, PM at beg and halfway point—162 (182, 202, 222, 242, 262, 282) sts.

Row 1: *k12 (13, 16, 17, 18, 21, 22), m1 right leaning, k1 (mark st), m1 left leaning, k12 (14, 15, 17, 19, 20, 22), double decrease, k12 (14, 15, 17, 19, 20, 22), m1 right leaning, k1 (mark st), m1 left leaning, k12 (14, 15, 17, 19, 20, 22), double decrease, k12 (14, 15, 17, 19, 20, 22), m1 right leaning, k1 (mark st), m1 left leaning, k12 (13, 16, 17, 18, 21, 22)*. Rep from * to * on second half of skirt. You will have formed 3 peaks (m1, k1, m1) on each front and back of skirt.

Row 2: knit.

Row 3: k, inc before and after 7 marked inc sts from Row 1 by: m1 right leaning, k1, m1 left leaning.

Row 4: knit.

Row 5: *k13 (14, 17, 18, 19, 22, 23), m1 right leaning, k1, m1 left leaning, k13 (14, 17, 18, 19, 22, 23), k3tog, k13 (14, 17, 18, 19, 22, 23), m1 right leaning, k1, m1 left leaning, k13 (14, 17, 18, 19, 22, 23), k3tog, k13 (14, 17, 18, 19, 22, 23), m1 right leaning, k1, m1 left leaning, k13 (14, 17, 18, 19, 22, 23)*. Rep from * to * on second half of skirt.

Row 6: knit.

Work rows 1–6, twice. Inc before and after the marked st, the st count will cont to change as the flare grows.

Work rows 3 and 4, 3 times. P 1 row.

Work St st 1.5".

BO: *k2tog, put newly made st from right needle back onto left needle,* rep from * to * around.

Fold hem up to WS at p row and sew into place.

finishing

Fold top over at p row. Sew CO top along inside to form casing for elastic waistband. Leave 2" space for opening, feed in elastic. Fit elastic to correct length. Secure elastic. Finish closing casing.

pure cables cardigan set

BY TAMARA DEL SONNO

This stylish soy cardigan set is covered in kicky cables that set off the yarn's natural beauty. If you are more the jeans-and-a-hoodie type, knit just the heavily cabled shell, which is absolutely lovely to wear year round.

SIZE

XS (S, M, L, 1X, 2X, 3X)

(It is shown here in size large.)

Bust 28–30 (32–34, 36–38, 40–42, 44–46, 48–50, 52–54)"

FINISHED MEASUREMENTS

Shell (chest): 31 (34, 38, 42, 46, 50, 54)"

Cardigan (chest): 34 (38, 42, 46, 50, 54, 58)"

Skirt (hip): 30 (34, 38, 42, 46, 50, 54)"

MATERIALS

South West Trading Company Pure (100% SoySilk soy fiber, 150 m per 50 g skein); color: #074 Wistful; shell: 2 (2, 3, 3, 3, 4) skeins; cardigan: 5 (5, 6, 6, 7, 7) skeins; skirt: 4 (4, 4, 5, 5, 6) skeins

Shell: 24" U.S. #4/3.5 mm circular needle and 24" U.S. #5/3.75 mm circular needle

Cardigan: 24" U.S. #7/4.5 mm circular needle and 24" U.S. #8/5 mm circular needle

Skirt: 24" U.S. #7/4.5 mm circular needle and 24" U.S. #8/5 mm circular needle

Cable needle

Stitch holders

Removable stitch markers

1" nonroll elastic, desired length around waist, for waistband

Large-eyed, blunt needle

Coordinating thread

GAUGE

Shell: 24 sts and 26 rows = 4" in cable pattern, U.S. #5

Cardigan: 22 sts and 25 rows = 4" in stockinette stitch, U.S. #8

Skirt: 22 sts and 25 rows = 4" in stockinette stitch, U.S. #8

A note on gauge: Knit a sample square using the given needle sizes before moving on to the entire project. Knitters who knit even a tiny bit loosely may find they want to move down a needle size to give the fabric more body and the cables more pop. This is especially true on the skirt, where relatively firm fabric is a good thing for durability's (and modesty's) sake!

PATTERN NOTES

Cable Pattern Sizes XS (L, XL, 2X, 3X)

Rows 1, 3, 5, and 7: *k2, p2, k4, p2, k2, p2, k6, p2; rep from * to end of row.

Rows 2, 4, 6, and 8: work the sts as they appear.

Row 9 (RS): *k2, p2, k4, p2, k2, p2, k6, p2; rep from * to end of row.

Rows 10, 12, 14, and 16: work the sts as they appear.

Row 11: *k2, p2, k4, p2, k2, p2, C6F, p2; rep from * to end of row.

continued

Row 13: *k2, p2, k4, p2, k2, p2, k6, p2; rep from * to end of row.

Row 15: *k2, p2, C4F, p2, k2, p2, k6, p2; rep from * to end of row.

Rows 17–24: rep rows 9–16.

Size S

Rows 1, 3, 5, and 7: *k2, p2, k1, p2, k2, k6, p2, k2, p2, k4, p2, k2, k6, p2; rep from * to last st, k1.

Rows 2, 4, 6, and 8: work the sts as they appear.

Row 9 (RS): k2, p2, k1, p2, k2, p2, k6, p2, *k2, p2, k4, p2, k2, p2, k6, p2; rep from * to end of row.

Rows 10, 12, 14, and 16: work the sts as they appear.

Row 11: *k2, p2, k1, p2, k2, p2, C6F, p2; rep from * to end of row.

Row 13: *k2, p2, k1, p2, k2, p2, k6, p2; rep from * to end of row.

Row 15: k2, p2, k1, p2, k2, p2, k6, p2, *k2, p2, C4F, p2, k6, p2; rep from * to end of row.

Rows 17–24: rep rows 9–16.

Size M

Rows 1, 3, 5, and 7: k2, p1, k4, p2, k2, p2, k6, p2, *k2, p2, k4, p2, k2, p2, k6, p2; rep from * to end of row.

Rows 2, 4, 6, and 8: work the sts as they appear.

Row 9 (RS): k2, p1, k4, p2, k2, p2, k6, p2, *k2, p2, k4, p2, k2, p2, k6, p2; rep from * to end of row.

Rows 10, 12, 14, and 16: work the sts as they appear.

Row 11: *k2, p1, k4, p2, k2, p2, C6F, p2; rep from * to end of row.

Row 13: *k2, p1, k4, p2, k2, p2, k6, p2; rep from * to end of row.

Row 15: *k2, p1, C4F, p2, k2, p2, k6, p2; rep from * to end of row.

Rows 17–24: rep rows 9–16.

SPECIAL ABBREVIATIONS

C6F: slip 3 stitches onto cable needle, hold at front of work, knit 3, knit 3 stitches from cable needle.

C4F: slip 2 stitches onto cable needle, hold at front of work, knit 2, knit 2 stitches from cable needle.

Pure Cables

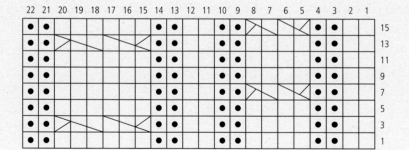

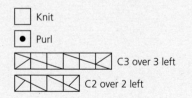

□ Knit
● Purl
C3 over 3 left
C2 over 2 left

shell directions

BACK

Using #5 needle, CO 98 (110, 120, 130, 142, 152, 164) sts and work 16 rows of cable pattern.

Cont working rows 9–16 of cable pattern as established until the back measures 9 (10, 10, 11, 11, 12, 13)" or desired length to underarm. BO 4 (4, 5, 5, 6, 6, 7) sts at beg of next 2 rows. Dec 1 st at beg and end of RS row 3 (3, 4, 4, 5, 5, 6) times—84 (100, 102, 112, 120, 130, 138) sts.

Cont in established patt until work measures 1 (1, 1, 1.5, 1.5, 1.5)" shorter than desired total length.

SHOULDERS

Work across 26 (31, 32, 35, 38, 41, 44) sts, turn, dec 1 st at neck edge every other row, 3 times. Work 2 more rows. Place these 23 (28, 29, 32, 36, 38, 41) sts on holder.

Loosely BO center 32 (38, 38, 42, 44, 48, 50) neck sts.

SECOND SHOULDER

Work across 25 (30, 31, 34, 37, 40, 43) sts. Dec 1 st at neck edge every other row, 3 times. Work 2 more rows. Place these 23 (28, 29, 32, 36, 38, 41) sts on holder.

FRONT

Work as for Back until 1 row after last dec above underarm BO.

Divide into 2 sections at center CF6, and work separately.

LEFT SIDE

Row 1 (RS): k3, dec 1 st, work in patt to end of row.

Row 2: as established.

Rep rows 1 and 2 until 29 (34, 36, 38, 42, 44, 47) sts rem, then work as established until length matches back. Place sts on holder.

RIGHT SIDE

Row 1 (RS): work in patt to last 5 sts, dec 1 st, k3.

Row 2: as established.

Rep rows 1 and 2 until 29 (34, 36, 38, 42, 44, 47) sts rem, then work as established until length matches back. Place sts on holder.

finishing

Join shoulder seams. Reserve 3 sts at front edge on holder. Match shoulder sts to corresponding sts on back, work 3-needle bind off over shoulder sts. K3 reserved sts until long enough on both sides to meet at back center. Graft or 3-needle bind off tog. Attach to back neckline edge. Tuck in ends.

ARM EDGES

Using #4 needle, with RS facing, and starting at center underarm, pu sts along armhole edge, based on *2 sts for every 3 rows, then 3 sts for every 4 rows*, along entire edge. Work rib (k2, p2) for 5 rows. BO loosely, in patt. Sew side seams.

cardigan sweater directions

BACK

Using #7 needle, CO 98 (110, 120, 130, 142, 152,164) sts and work the 16 rows of cable pattern; rep rows 9–16 until work measures 5" or desired length. Change to #8 needle and work in St st until work measures 12 (12, 13, 14, 14, 15, 16)" or desired length to underarm.

BO 3 (4, 5, 5, 6, 7, 7) sts at beg of next 2 rows. Dec 1 st at beg and end of RS row 3 (3, 4, 4, 5, 5, 6) times—92 (96, 102, 112, 120, 128, 134) sts.

Cont in St st to 7 (7.5, 8, 8.5, 9, 9.5, 10)" or 1" less than desired length for underarm.

SHOULDERS

Work across 32 (34, 36, 39, 41, 44, 46) sts, turn, dec 1 st at neck edge every other row, 3 times. Work 2 more rows. Place these 29 (31, 33, 36, 38, 41, 43) sts on holder; break yarn.

BO loosely the center 28 (28, 30, 34, 38, 40, 42) sts for back neck edge.

SECOND SHOULDER

Attach yarn and work across 32 (34, 36, 39, 41, 44, 46) sts. Dec 1 st at neck edge every other row, 3 times. Work 2 more rows. Place these 29 (31, 33, 36, 38, 41, 43) sts on holder.

LEFT FRONT

Using #7 needle, CO 50 (56, 60, 66, 72, 76, 82) sts and work in cable pattern to 5" or same length as pattern section of back.

Change to #8 needle.

Row 1: work 10 sts in cable pattern and the rest of the row in St st.

Row 2: as established.

Cont in this manner, working 10 sts in patt and the rest of the rows in St st until work measures 12 (12, 13, 14, 14, 15, 16)" or desired length to underarm.

BO 3 (4, 5, 5, 6, 7, 7) sts at beg of RS. Dec 1 st at beg of RS row 3 (3, 4, 4, 5, 5, 6) times. At same time, k2tog at neck edge every 4th row, before commencing cable pattern 10 sts along.

Cont working in established patt, dec every 4th row at neck edge until 39 (41, 43, 46, 48, 51, 53) sts rem and the front is the same length as the back armhole. Reserve 10 sts in cable pattern at front edge on holder. Match shoulder sts to correspond-

ing sts on back and work 3-needle bind off over shoulder sts.

RIGHT FRONT

Work as for Left Front, reversing the shaping.

NECKLINE EDGE

Work across each set of 10 cable sts, keep in patt and attach along back neck edges to meet in center back of neck. Graft or 3-needle bind off sts tog at center back.

SLEEVES

Using #7 needle, CO 56 (58, 62, 64, 66, 68, 72) sts and work in cable pattern for 3". Begin inc 1 st at beg and end of row every 4th row, on RS, while cont cable pattern to 5", or desired length.

Change to #8 needle and work in St st, cont inc 1 st at beg and end of row every 4th row, on RS, until work measures 15 (15.5, 16, 16.5, 17, 17. 5, 18)" or to desired length to underarm.

BO 3 (4, 4, 5, 6, 7, 8) sts at beg of next 2 rows. Dec 3 sts at beg of next 4 rows. Dec 1 st at beg and end of each row 3 times. Work even 1 (2, 2.5, 3, 3.5, 4, 4.5)". BO 4 sts at beg of next 2 rows. BO 6 sts at beg of next 2 rows. BO 8 sts at beg of next 2 rows. BO rem sts.

finishing

Ease sleeves into armhole, sew underarm seams. Sew body side seams. Tuck in ends.

skirt directions

Using #7 needle, CO 180 (212, 234, 256, 278, 300, 322) sts and work in cable pattern as established for size XS until 5" or 6", or desired length of patt on skirt.

Change to #8 needle.

Join to work in rnd: On the RS, k to last 12 sts, place holder to weave under for kick pleat at finishing. Work cable pattern over 12 sts of left top of kick pleat for next 2" or beg St st immediately, as desired.

Divide skirt sts in half, with the kick pleat in the center back. Place st markers at each side seam for later shaping. Work in St st for 20"–24" or desired length to hip. Dec 20 sts, evenly spaced around. Work 2" even. Dec 20 sts, evenly spaced around. Work 2" even.

P 1 rnd. Change to #7 needle. Knit 1.25". BO using k2tog, put st back on left needle, around.

finishing

Fold over at p row. Sew BO top along inside to form casing for elastic waistband. Leave 2" space opening, feed in elastic. Fit elastic to correct length. Secure elastic. Finish closing casing.

At bottom, weave the sts from the holder loosely into the inside of the cable edge to create walking vent. Sew in ends. Enjoy!

midnight lace stole

BY SIVIA HARDING

This cleverly constructed beaded shawl goes with everything from jeans to an evening gown. Made of Sea Silk yarn (which is part silk and part seaweed), it has an elegant drape and sheen. If you've never tried beaded knitting before, you'll quickly become addicted.

SIZE

One size fits all.

FINISHED MEASUREMENTS

Dimensions: 70" x 21"

MATERIALS

Handmaiden Fine Yarn Sea Silk (70% silk, 30% seacell; 400 m per 100 g skein); color: Midnight; 3 skeins

24" U.S. #3/3.25 mm circular needle

392 seed beads, size 8/0

Dental-floss threader or big-eyed beading needle

Stitch markers

Tapestry needle

GAUGE

22 sts and 34 rows = 4" in stockinette stitch, after blocking

SPECIAL ABBREVIATIONS

B (place bead): slide bead as close as possible to right needle, leaving bead on strand between 2 stitches.

k3tog: knit 3 together.

LLI (left lifted increase): insert the left-hand needle from front to back under the left leg of the stitch two rows below the first stitch on the right-hand needle, lifting this loop onto the left-hand needle, then knit into this loop to create a new stitch.

RLI (right lifted increase): knit into the top of the stitch below the first stitch on the left-hand needle, leaving the first stitch on the left-hand needle.

sl1-k2tog-psso: slip a stitch as if to knit, knit 2 together, pass slipped stitch over k2tog.

tbl: through back loop.

syif: slip 1 stitch with yarn in front.

PATTERN NOTES

Beads must be strung onto yarn before knitting starts. The stole shown uses sparkling magenta-lined amethyst ab 8/0 triangles from Earth Faire. Dental-floss threaders for stringing beads are cheap and easy to find in drugstores. (People use them to thread floss around their braces and bridges.) These threaders are made of semi-rigid plastic; each has a loop at one end and a needle-like tip at the other. To use one for stringing beads onto yarn, pass the yarn through its loop, pick up beads with its needle-like tip, and slide the beads over the loop and onto the yarn.

continued

Midnight Lace Pattern (panel of 15 sts)

Row 1: (k2tog, k1, yo, k1) twice, yo, k1, ssk, k1, yo, k1, ssk.

Rows 2, 4, 6, and 8: purl.

Row 3: yo, ssk, k1, k2tog, k1, yo, k3, yo, k1, ssk, k1, k2tog, yo.

Row 5: p1, yo, k3tog, k1, yo, k5, yo, k1, sl1-k2tog-psso, yo, p1.

Row 7: p1, k2tog, k1, yo, k7, yo, k1, ssk, p1.

Rep rows 1–8 for pattern.

Arrow Lace Pattern (panel of 7 sts)

Row 1: yo, ssk, k3, k2tog, yo.

Rows 2, 4, 6, and 8: purl.

Row 3: k1, yo, ssk, k1, k2tog, yo, k1.

Row 5: k2, yo, sl1-k2tog-psso, yo, k2.

Row 7: ssk, k1, yo, k1, yo, k1, k2tog.

Rep rows 1–8 for pattern.

Lace Column Pattern (panel of 3 sts)

Row 1 (RS): yo, sl1-k2tog-psso, yo.

Row 2 (WS): purl.

Rep rows 1 and 2 for pattern.

Midnight Lace

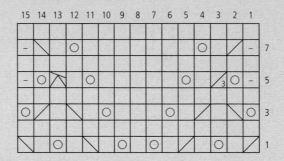

Arrow Lace

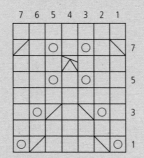

Lace Column

☐	Knit 1 on RS, purl 1 on WS
–	Purl 1 on RS, knit 1 on WS
╱	Knit 2 together
╲	Ssk (slip, slip, knit)
○	Yarn over
⧄	Slip 1, k2tog, psso

directions

CENTER PANEL

Thread 168 beads onto yarn with dental-floss threader or big-eyed beading needle. CO 33 sts and k 5 rows (garter st).

Row 1 (RS): k1, k1 tbl, p1, B, p1, arrow lace pattern over 7 sts, p1, B, p1, yo, k2tog, yo, k3, yo, ssk, yo, p1, B, p1, arrow lace pattern over 7 sts, p1, B, p1, k1 tbl, k1—35 sts.

Row 2 and all even-numbered rows in this section: purl.

Row 3: k1, k1 tbl, p2, arrow lace pattern over 7 sts, p2, yo, k2tog, yo, k5, yo, ssk, yo, p2, arrow lace pattern over 7 sts, p2, k1 tbl, k1—37 sts.

Row 5: k1, k1 tbl, p1, B, p1, arrow lace pattern over 7 sts, p1, B, p1, yo, k2tog, yo, k7, yo, ssk, yo, p1, B, p1, arrow lace pattern over 7 sts, p1, B, p1, k1 tbl, k1—39 sts.

Row 7: k1, k1 tbl, p2, arrow lace pattern over 7 sts, p2, yo, k2tog, yo, k9, yo, ssk, yo, p2, arrow lace pattern over 7 sts, p2, k1 tbl, k1—41 sts.

Row 9: k1, k1 tbl, p1, B, p1, arrow lace pattern over 7 sts, p1, B, p1, yo, k2tog, yo, k2, ssk, k1, yo, k1, yo, k1, ssk, k2, yo, ssk, yo, p1, B, p1, arrow lace pattern over 7 sts, p1, B, p1, k1 tbl, k1—43 sts.

Row 11: k1, k1 tbl, p2, arrow lace pattern over 7 sts, p2, yo, k2tog, yo, k2, ssk, k1, yo, k3, yo, k1, ssk, k2, yo, ssk, yo, p2, arrow lace pattern over 7 sts, p2, k1 tbl, k1—45 sts.

Row 13: k1, k1 tbl, p1, B, p1, arrow lace pattern over 7 sts, p1, B, p1, yo, k2tog, yo, k2, ssk, k1, yo, k5, yo, k1, ssk, k2, yo, ssk, yo, p1, B, p1, arrow lace pattern over 7 sts, p1, B, p1, k1 tbl, k1—47 sts.

Row 15: k1, k1 tbl, p2, arrow lace pattern over 7 sts, p2, yo, k2tog, yo, k2, ssk, k1, yo, k7, yo, k1, ssk, k2, yo, ssk, yo, p2, arrow lace pattern over 7 sts, p2, k1 tbl, k1—49 sts.

Row 17: k1, k1 tbl, p2, arrow lace pattern over 7 sts, p2, yo, k2tog, yo, k9, yo, ssk, yo, p2, arrow lace pattern over 7 sts, p2, k1 tbl, k1—51 sts.

Row 19: k1, k1 tbl, p1, B, p1, arrow lace pattern over 7 sts, p1, B, p1, yo, k2tog, yo, k2, midnight lace pattern over 15 sts, k2, yo, ssk, yo, p1, B, p1, arrow lace pattern over 7 sts, p1, B, p1, k1 tbl, k1—53 sts.

Row 21: k1, k1 tbl, p2, arrow lace pattern over 7 sts, p2, yo, sl1-k2tog-psso, yo, k2, midnight lace pattern over 15 sts, k2, yo, sl1-k2tog-psso, yo, p2, arrow lace pattern over 7 sts, p2, k1 tbl, k1.

Row 23: k1, k1 tbl, p1, B, p1, arrow lace pattern over 7 sts, p1, B, p1, yo, sl1-k2tog-psso, yo, k2, midnight lace pattern over 15 sts, k2, yo, sl1-k2tog-psso, yo, p1, B, p1, arrow lace pattern over 7 sts, p1, B, p1, k1 tbl, k1.

Row 25: rep Row 21.

Row 27: k1, k1 tbl, p1, B, p1, arrow lace pattern over 7 sts, p1, B, p1, PM, LLI, PM, yo, k2tog, yo, k2, SM, midnight lace pattern over 15 sts, SM, k2, yo, ssk, yo, PM, RLI, PM, p1, B, p1, arrow lace pattern over 7 sts, p1, B, p1, k1 tbl, k1—55 sts.

Row 29: k1, k1 tbl, p2, arrow lace pattern over 7 sts, p2, SM, k1, SM, yo, sl1-k2tog-psso, yo, k2, SM, midnight lace pattern over 15 sts, SM, k2, yo, sl1-k2tog-psso, yo, SM, k1, SM, p2, arrow lace pattern over 7 sts, p2, k1 tbl, k1.

Row 31: k1, k1 tbl, p1, B, p1, arrow lace pattern over 7 sts, p1, B, p1, SM, k1, SM, yo, sl1-k2tog-psso, yo, k2, SM, midnight lace pattern over 15 sts, SM, k2, yo, sl1-k2tog-psso, yo, SM, k1, SM, p1, B, p1, arrow lace pattern over 7 sts, p1, B, p1, k1 tbl, k1.

Row 33: rep Row 29.

Establish patt rep as follows:

Row 35: k1, k1 tbl, p1, B, p1, arrow lace pattern over 7 sts, p1, B, p1, SM, k1, LLI, k to marker, SM, yo, k2tog, yo, k2, SM, midnight lace pattern over 15 sts, SM, k2, yo, ssk, yo, SM, k to 1 st before marker, RLI, k1, SM, p1, B, p1, arrow lace pattern over 7 sts, p1, B, p1, k1 tbl, k1—57 sts.

Row 37: k1, k1 tbl, p2, arrow lace pattern over 7 sts, p2, SM, k to next marker, SM, yo, sl1-k2tog-psso, yo, k2, SM, midnight lace pattern over 15 sts, SM, k2, yo, sl1-k2tog-psso, yo, SM, k to next marker, SM, p2, arrow lace pattern over 7 sts, p2, k1 tbl, k1.

Row 39: k1, k1 tbl, p1, B, p1, arrow lace pattern over 7 sts, p1, B, p1, SM, yo, sl1-k2tog-psso, yo, k2, SM, k to next marker, SM, midnight lace pattern over 15 sts, SM, k2, yo, sl1-k2tog-psso, yo, SM, k to next marker, SM, p1, B, p1, arrow lace patt over 7 sts, p1, B, p1, k1 tbl, k1.

Row 41: rep Row 37.

Rep rows 35–41 for patt. Continuing in established patt, inc 2 sts on each Row 35 for a total of 15 times, ending on a Row 41—85 sts.

K 5 rows (garter st). BO loosely. Do not cut yarn. Leave st resulting from last bound-off st on needle.

RIGHT SIDE PANEL

With RS facing and beg at the bottom edge, pu and k108 sts along right edge of center panel (approx 2 out of every 3 edge sts)—109 sts. Turn. With WS facing, k3, p to last 3 sts, k3.

Beg with the next RS row, establish patt as follows:

Row 1: k3, *yo, sl1-k2tog-psso, yo, p1, midnight lace pattern over 15 sts, p1, rep from * to last 6 sts, yo, sl1-k2tog-psso, yo, k3.

Row 2 and all even-numbered rows: k3, p to last 3 sts, k3.

Rep rows 1 and 2 until the 8-row midnight lace pattern has been worked a total of 23 times.

SHORT ROWS

Short rows will allow you to inc the length of the bottom edge of the side panel. These are worked in 8-row increments across each rep of the lace pattern along the side of the stole.

Row 1: k3, *yo, sl1-k2tog-psso, yo, p1, midnight lace pattern over 15 sts, p1, rep from * 4 times, yo, sl1-k2tog-psso, yo, p1, work 15 sts of midnight lace pattern as set, wrap and turn.

Row 2 and all even-numbered rows up until Row 32: p to last 3 sts, k3.

Row 3: k3, *yo, sl1-k2tog-psso, yo, p1, midnight lace pattern over 15 sts, p1, rep from * 4 times, yo, sl1-k2tog-psso, yo, p1, work 11 sts of midnight lace pattern as set, wrap and turn.

Row 5: k3, *yo, sl1-k2tog-psso, yo, p1, midnight lace pattern over 15 sts, p1, rep from * 4 times, yo, sl1-k2tog-psso, yo, p1, work 7 sts of midnight lace pattern as set, wrap and turn.

Row 7: k3, *yo, sl1-k2tog-psso, yo, p1, midnight lace pattern over 15 sts, p1, rep from * 4 times, yo, sl1-k2tog-psso, yo, p1, work 3 sts of midnight lace pattern as set, wrap and turn.

Rows 9–15: work as for rows 1–7, completing 3 reps of the midnight lace pattern before the partial section and wrap and turn.

Rows 17–23: work as for rows 1–7, completing 2 reps of the midnight lace pattern before the partial section and wrap and turn.

Rows 25–31: work as for rows 1–7, completing 1 rep of the midnight lace pattern before the partial section and wrap and turn.

Row 32 (RS): syif, k across entire row, picking up wraps and working them tog with the sts they were wrapping, and at the same time inc 4 sts evenly across the row—113 sts.

Row 33 (WS): syif, p across row.

BEADED EDGING

String 112 beads onto a new ball of yarn or the other end of your working yarn, being sure to string a few extra beads. The edging is worked perpendicular to the stole and requires CO additional sts. The following rows are worked over these sts. One st from the stole edge is worked tog with one st from the edging at the end of each RS row, advancing the edging across the row, until all stole sts have been used.

Using the beaded ball, attach yarn at working edge of stole with RS facing. CO 23 sts.

Row 1 (RS): k to last CO st, ssk (1 st from the edging tog with 1 st from the stole).

Row 2 and all even-numbered rows in this section (WS): sl1 st pwise, p to last edging st, k1.

Row 3: k1, (yo, k2tog) 5 times, yo, k1, p1, B, p1, arrow lace pattern over 7 sts, p1, B, p2tog (1 st from the edging tog with 1 st from the stole).

Row 5: k1, (yo, k2tog) 5 times, yo, k2, p2, arrow lace pattern over 7 sts, p1, p2tog (1 st from the edging tog with 1 st from the stole).

Row 7: k1, (yo, k2tog) 5 times, yo, k3, p1, B, p1, arrow lace pattern over 7 sts, p1, B, p2tog (1 st from the edging tog with 1 st from the stole).

Row 9: k1, (yo, k2tog) 5 times, yo, k4, p2, arrow lace pattern over 7 sts, p1, p2tog (1 st from the edging tog with 1 st from the stole).

Row 11: k1, (yo, k2tog) 5 times, yo, k5, p1, B, p1, arrow lace pattern over 7 sts, p1, B,

Beaded Edging

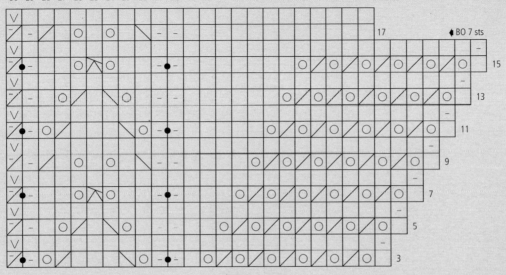

	Knit 1 on RS, purl 1 on WS			Yarn over
-	Purl 1 on RS, knit 1 on WS		⧄	Slip 1, k2tog, psso
⟋	Knit 2 together		⟋	Purl 2 together
⟍	Ssk (slip, slip, knit)		V	Slip 1 st purlwise
●	Bead: slide bead as close as possible to right needle, leaving bead on strand between 2 sts			

p2tog (1 st from the edging tog with 1 st from the stole).

Row 13: k1, (yo, k2tog) 5 times, yo, k6, p2, arrow lace pattern over 7 sts, p1, p2tog (1 st from the edging tog with 1 st from the stole).

Row 15: k1, (yo, k2tog) 5 times, yo, k7, p1, B, p1, arrow lace pattern over 7 sts, p1, B, p2tog (1 st from the edging tog with 1 st from the stole).

Row 17: BO 7 sts loosely, k11 (12 sts on needle), p2, arrow lace pattern over 7 sts, p1, p2tog (1 st from the edging tog with 1 st from the stole).

Rep rows 3–18 until all stole sts have been used. After final Row 18, BO edging sts loosely in k.

LEFT SIDE PANEL

With RS facing and beg at the top edge, attach a new ball of yarn and pu and k109 sts along left edge of center panel (approx 2 out of every 3 edge sts). Turn. With WS facing, k3, p to last 3 sts, k3. Continue as for right side panel up to the short-row section.

SHORT ROWS

Short rows will allow you to inc the length of the bottom edge of the side panel. These are worked in 8-row increments across each rep of the lace pattern along the side of the stole.

Row 1: k3, *yo, sl1-k2tog-psso, yo, p1, midnight lace pattern over 15 sts, p1, rep from * 4 times, yo, sl1-k2tog-psso, yo, p1, work 15 sts of midnight lace pattern as set, wrap and turn.

Row 2 and all even-numbered rows in this section: p to last 3 sts, k3.

Row 3: Row 1: k3, *yo, sl1-k2tog-psso, yo, p1, midnight lace pattern over 15 sts, p1, rep from * 4 times, yo, sl1-k2tog-psso, yo, p1, work 11 sts of midnight lace pattern as set, wrap and turn.

Row 5: Row 1: k3, *yo, sl1-k2tog-psso, yo, p1, midnight lace pattern over 15 sts, p1, rep from * 4 times, yo, sl1-k2tog-psso, yo, p1, work 7 sts of midnight lace pattern as set, wrap and turn.

Row 7: Row 1: k3, *yo, sl1-k2tog-psso, yo, p1, midnight lace pattern over 15 sts, p1, rep from * 4 times, yo, sl1-k2tog-psso, yo, p1, work 3 sts of midnight lace pattern as set, wrap and turn.

Rows 9–15: work as for rows 1–7, completing 3 reps of the midnight lace pattern before the partial section and wrap and turn.

Rows 17–23: work as for rows 1–7, completing 2 reps of the midnight lace pattern before the partial section and wrap and turn.

Rows 25–31: work as for rows 1–7, completing 1 rep of the midnight lace pattern before the partial section and wrap and turn.

Next RS row: syif, knit across entire row, picking up wraps and working them tog with the sts they were wrapping, and at the same time increasing 3 sts evenly across the row—112 sts.

Next WS row: syif, purl across row.

BEADED EDGING

String 112 beads onto a new ball of yarn or the other end of your working yarn, being sure to string a few extra beads. The edging is worked perpendicular to the stole and requires casting on additional sts. The following rows are worked over these sts. One st from the stole edge is worked tog with one st from the edging at the end of each RS row, advancing the edging across the row, until all stole sts have been used.

Using the beaded ball, attach yarn at working edge of stole with RS facing. CO 23 sts.

Row 1 (RS): k to last CO st, ssk (1 st from the edging tog with 1 st from the stole).

Row 2 and all even-numbered rows in this section (WS): Sl1 st pwise, p to last edging st, k1.

Row 3: k1, (yo, k2tog) 5 times, yo, k1, p1, B, p1, arrow lace pattern over 7 sts, p1, B, p2tog (1 st from the edging tog with 1 st from the stole).

Row 5: k1, (yo, k2tog) 5 times, yo, k2, p2, arrow lace pattern over 7 sts, p1, p2tog (1 st from the edging tog with 1 st from the stole).

Row 7: k1, (yo, k2tog) 5 times, yo, k3, p1, B, p1, arrow lace pattern over 7 sts, p1, B, p2tog (1 st from the edging tog with 1 st from the stole).

Row 9: k1, (yo, k2tog) 5 times, yo, k4, p2, arrow lace pattern over 7 sts, p1, p2tog (1 st from the edging tog with 1 st from the stole).

Row 11: k1, (yo, k2tog) 5 times, yo, k5, p1, B, p1, arrow lace pattern over 7 sts, p1, B,

p2tog (1 st from the edging tog with 1 st from the stole).

Row 13: k1, (yo, k2tog) 5 times, yo, k6, p2, arrow lace pattern over 7 sts, p1, p2tog (1 st from the edging tog with 1 st from the stole).

Row 15: k1, (yo, k2tog) 5 times, yo, k7, p1, B, p1, arrow lace pattern over 7 sts, p1, B, p2tog (1 st from the edging tog with 1 st from the stole).

Row 17: BO 7 sts loosely, k11 (12 sts on needle), p2, arrow lace pattern over 7 sts, p1, p2tog (1 st from the edging tog with 1 st from the stole).

Rep rows 3–18 until all stole sts have been used. After final Row 18, BO edging sts loosely in k.

finishing

Weave in all ends. Submerge garment in lukewarm water containing a few drops of wool wash, gently wrap in a towel, and block to given measurements. Allow to dry flat.

merian wrap

BY KERI WILLIAMS

I love scribble lace, as über-creative knit designer Debbie New calls this type of stitch pattern. Even just the name sounds fun, and I'm a big fan of the wavy lines the different yarns make. Add luscious fibers and big needles, and the knitting just flows off the needles into a large piece of lightweight luxury. If you'd rather use circular needles, substitute a 24" U.S. #15/10 mm circular for the two sets of straight needles.

SIZE

One size fits all.

FINISHED MEASUREMENTS

Dimensions: 23" x 60"

MATERIALS

Color A: Habu tsumugi (100% silk; 450 yd/402 m per 48 g skein); color: #48; 1 skein

Color B: Alchemy Silken Straw (100% silk; 236 yd/215 m per 40 g skein); color: Amethyst; 1 skein

Color C: Undyed silk hankies (100% silk; 50 g)

U.S. #15/10 mm straight needles

U.S. #13/9 mm straight needles

Darning needle

GAUGE

Gauge is not critical to this pattern as long as the fabric you are creating pleases you!

PATTERN NOTES

Color Pattern
   Row 1: Color A
   Row 2: Color B
   Row 3: Color C
   Row 4: Color B

When working scribble lace, you will come to a point when the working end of the next color is at the non–working end of the needle. If you are using straight needles, slide the piece onto the smaller needles, then work it back onto the larger needles, keeping the knit and purl orientation. If you are using a circular needle, just slide the piece so the working end for the next color is at the working end of the needle, keeping the knit and purl orientation.

YARN NOTES

Working with silk hankies is a lot of fun. Peel off as fine a layer as possible from a silk hankie. With your thumbs punch a hole in the middle of the silk hankie layer, and draw the hankie into a loop. Continue to draw the hankie until you achieve the thickness you desire. Break the loop at a weak point. To join silk hankie strands, lay the new end on top of the working strand and lightly rub together. The amount required for silk hankies is an estimate only. The exact quantity required depends on the thickness of the strands you create.

Knitting this piece works best on wooden needles with a reasonably pointy tip. Metal needles are too slippery, and bamboo needles can sometimes catch the fine silk fibers. Silken straw can split if the needles have too sharp a point.

directions

With A, CO 130 sts very loosely.

In color pattern, work St st.

Work patt until piece measures 22", ending with an A row.

Work one more row in A.

Break A yarn 140" from end of piece.

BO, using sewn bind-off method. To make
a sewn bind off, break a long piece of rem
yarn and sew from the front into the center
of the next st, coming through from back to
front before entering the next st to the left,
and cont to move across from right to left.

Using A, on the end of the piece with RS
facing, pu and k62 sts. In St st, work 7
rows. BO using sewn bind-off method. Rep
for other end.

finishing

Weave in loose ends.

sea creature möbius necklet

BY SHANNON OKEY

I love Cat Bordhi's Möbius work (check out catbordhi.com for her *Treasuries of Magical Knitting*)—Möbius strips are truly magical! This piece, with one edge and one surface, is knit entirely in the round; you'll love the drape and look of this unique scarf.

SIZE
One size fits all.

FINISHED MEASUREMENTS
Dimensions: varies depending on your choices below

MATERIALS
Tilli Tomas Soie de la Mer (70% silk, 30% seaweed; 260 yd per 100 g skein); color: Coral Sap; 1 skein (or more if you choose to go larger)

47" U.S. #9/5.5 mm circular needle

Tapestry needle

GAUGE
Gauge is not critical to this pattern.

PATTERN NOTES
If you like the idea of shimmering jewels studding the surface of your scarf and lots of extra texture, try alternating rows with a skein of Tilli Tomas Cleopatra Ribbon, a silk ribbon yarn pre-beaded with chunky glass beads. In fact, any of the Tilli Tomas beaded yarns would look great here, or choose to include your own beads using the techniques in Sivia Harding's Midnight Lace Stole (page 57).

The Möbius cast on has been demonstrated in many places, among them Cat Bordhi's books and the television show *Knitty Gritty*. It really is easier to understand if you watch it in action. Toward that end, Cat will be releasing a free video demonstrating the cast on on YouTube.com.

directions

Using Möbius CO, create slipknot and curl your needle to accept the sts starting in the center of the circular needle's cable. CO sts until you have covered the needle (approx 200).

K first few rnds, being careful to maintain an even tension. If you've opted to include a beaded ribbon yarn as suggested above, wait until you've knit these first few rnds so as not to disrupt your tension. The initial series of rnds are sometimes tricky to complete, but once done, it's all straight knitting!

SEA CREATURE SLUBS

Periodically, create a knitted "slub" with short rows as follows:

Rnd 1: choose a place to create slub and *wyif, sl1, wyib place st back on left needle, turn.

Rnd 2: p across a random number of sts, wrap and turn*.

Rnds 3+: k, rep from * to * as many times as you'd like.

Keeping the slubs' locations random and the number of stitches chosen random will add to the effect, and these short-row slubs will bulge out appealingly from the knitted surface, giving extra texture and dimension to your knitting. You can also throw in a few random increases and decreases, or even bobbles, over the body of the slub to make it even more textural. Think of yourself as a sculptor!

When scarf is to your desired dimensions or you are running out of yarn, BO. Remember, there are twice as many sts as it appears there are! You will need more yarn to BO than you might expect.

finishing

Weave in ends.

phoenix quick wrap

BY KATE JACKSON

This is truly a quick and appealing knit for when you need that certain *je ne sais quoi* to spice up an outfit. Two buttonholes make the wrap size adjustable. It's fast, it's fun, and it looks great on everyone.

SIZE

One size, easily adjusted up or down

FINISHED MEASUREMENTS

Shoulders: 32"

Length: 12.5"

MATERIALS

South West Trading Company Phoenix (100% SoySilk; 175 yd per 100 g skein); color: #506 Black; 2 balls

32" U.S. #10/6 mm circular needle

Button

Sewing needle

Coordinating thread

Tapestry needle

GAUGE

16 sts and 22 rows = 4" in stockinette stitch

directions

WRAP

Using a long-tail cast on, CO 35 sts.

Rows 1–4: knit.

Row 5 (WS): k2, p25, k8.

Rep the last 2 rows until piece measures 33", ending with a WS row.

K 3 rows even.

BO row (WS): (BO 5, fasten off the st on your right-hand needle by pulling the ball of yarn through it, drop the next st, and pull a short length of yarn to space the next set of bind offs about 1") 4 times. BO rem 11 sts.

TOP BAND

CO 8 sts, then pu and k105 sts along the top edge of the wrap. This is the side with only 2 sts in garter—113 sts.

K 5 rows.

Next row (RS): k2, yo, k2tog, k2, yo, k2tog, k to end.

K 3 rows.

Next row: k, dec 8 sts evenly across row.

BO.

finishing

Sew button onto the top band of the wrap, opposite the flap with buttonholes. Weave in ends.

summer pine shawl

BY ANDI SMITH

This crocheted shawl gives optimum impact for very little work. The stitch used is incredibly easy and there is only one row to the pattern. If you haven't learned how to crochet yet, now's your chance! If you cannot find Habu Textiles A-47 yarn, this pattern is suitable for just about any of Habu Textile's paper, linen, bamboo, or other tape- and ribbon-style yarns.

SIZE
One size fits all.

FINISHED MEASUREMENTS
Dimensions: approx 10" x 96"

MATERIALS
Habu Textiles A-47 (100% pine ribbon; 186 yd per 100 g skein); color: Natural; 1 skein

U.S. #4/E/3.5 mm crochet hook

Large-eyed, blunt needle

GAUGE
Gauge is not critical for this garment.

PATTERN NOTES
STC (split treble cluster)

Step 1: yo hook 2 times, insert hook into 4th ch from hook, yo, pull through ch and 1 loop (3 loops on hook), yo, pull through 2 loops on hook (2 loops rem on hook).

Step 2: rep step 1, then yo, pull through rem 3 loops.

YARN NOTES
Take care when winding this yarn into a ball—it is very fine and has a tendency to knot and twist on itself. Winding the fiber onto a wide ribbon spool prevents it from tangling while it is in use. The yarn arrives with a great deal of sizing, which initially creates a very stiff, inflexible fabric. Sizing, which is used to keep yarns stiff during weaving, will wash out! After finishing the shawl, rinse it in lukewarm water and a fiber conditioner such as SOAK to produce a wonderfully drapey, soft finish.

directions

Row 1: ch 406, turn.

Row 2: work step 1 of STC into 6th ch from hook, step 2 into following 4th ch, *ch 3, then step 1 of STC into same ch and step 2 into next 4th ch from hook. Rep from * to last ch. Work step 1 of STC, turn.

Row 3: ch 6, work STC, ch 3 across row ending with step 1 of STC in last ch.

Rep Row 3 until desired width is achieved.

finishing

Weave in ends along ch sts. Rinse shawl thoroughly and block into shape. Allow to dry completely before moving. Wrap in tissue to avoid creases in the shawl.

sjaal scarf

BY ANDI SMITH

Inspired by eighteenth-century Delft tiles, this scarf is super-quick to knit and a perfect Fair Isle project for beginners. The reverse side can be lined with coordinating fabric, which both hides all the carried yarn and provides an extra layer of warmth.

SIZE

One size fits all.

FINISHED MEASUREMENTS

Dimensions: approx 3.75" x 70"

MATERIALS

Crystal Palace Yarns Bamboozle (55% bamboo, 24% cotton, 21% elastic nylon; 90 yd/ 83 m per 50 g skein); color 1 (C1): #0204 Ivory, 2 skeins; color 2 (C2): #7063 Dutch Blue, 2 skeins

U.S. #9/5.5 mm straight needles

Large-eyed, blunt needle

Coordinating fabric and sewing thread (optional)

GAUGE

21 sts and 21 rows = 3.75" in stockinette stitch

PATTERN NOTES

When working with two or more colors, try not to carry any color more than 3 or 4 sts—it will alter the tension. It is simpler to use small skeins of yarn for a few sts.

This pattern is worked in stockinette stitch throughout; knit on the odd rows and purl on the even rows.

☐ Color 1 (C1)

▨ Color 2 (C2)

Central Panel

directions

With C1, CO 21 sts. Work 1 row in p and then follow the chart from rows 1–21 once and from rows 3–21, 17 times. BO in patt.

finishing

Be sure to weave in all ends securely. Match colors for weaving. Block by dampening and laying out to air-dry completely.

SCARF LINING (OPTIONAL)

After blocking, measure the scarf and cut a coordinating piece of fabric 1" larger. Pin into place, allowing a 0.5" seam allowance. Using thread that matches yarn color 1, whip st the fabric to the scarf 1 st in from the edges. This allows the scarf to wrap naturally around the fabric and creates a beautifully finished seam.

love-squared gauntlets

BY ANDI SMITH

These hand warmers were designed to keep my hands warm and my fingers free to knit in cold Ohio winters. The simple Fair Isle pattern lets the beauty of the color and yarn show through while the two-color rib really makes them stand out from the crowd. Everyone who sees these covets a pair of her own, including the book's photographer!

SIZE

S (M, L)

(It is shown here in size small.)

FINISHED MEASUREMENTS

Dimensions: 7" across the wrist; 6.5" from cuff to cuff. These hand warmers stretch about 1" with wear.

MATERIALS

Main color (MC): Crystal Palace Yarns Maizy (82% corn fiber, 18% elastic nylon; 204 yd per 50 g); color: #1208 Suede Tan; 1 skein

Contrasting color (CC): Crystal Palace Yarns Panda Cotton (55% bamboo, 24% cotton, 21% elastic nylon; 182 yd per 50 g); color: #9598 Jet Black; 1 skein

2 sets 24" U.S. #1/2.5 mm circular needles

2 stitch markers

Waste yarn or stitch holder

Large-eyed, blunt needle

GAUGE

40 sts and 44 rows = 4" in stockinette stitch

PATTERN NOTES

When working with two colors, be sure to carry your yarn at the back of your work. By carrying one yarn above and the other yarn below, the yarns will not twist too badly, but will still provide a secure bond to prevent holes in your work.

SPECIAL ABBREVIATIONS

kf: knit into the front

kb: knit into the back

YARN NOTES

Because both these yarns contain elastic, it's important not to stretch the work too much as you are knitting, but to find a comfortable tension. Working a gauge swatch will help you correct your tension, which is true of any multicolor stranded knitting but especially here. Like many yarns that are made up of multiple fibers, these yarns have a tendency to be a little splitty. Using metal needles and completely finishing each stitch before moving on to the next one greatly reduces splitting.

continued

Color Pattern

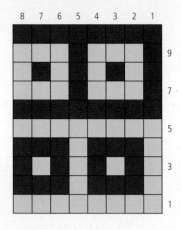

Main color (MC)

Contrasting color (CC)

directions

RIGHT-HAND CUFF

**Using long-tail CO method and MC, CO 64 (72, 80) sts.

Divide the sts onto the two needles, with 32 (36, 40) sts on each needle.

Being careful not to twist, work the ribbing as follows:

Rnd 1: With MC, k1, with CC, p1. Continue across the rnd, knitting with MC, and purling with CC. Remember to carry your yarns at the back of your work.

Rep Rnd 1 until cuff measures 1.5" or desired depth.

BODY

The body of the hand warmer is worked in k sts throughout.

Rnd 1: CC.

Rnd 2: (CC, k1, MC, k3), rep to end.

Rnd 3: (CC, k1, MC, k1), rep to end.

Rnd 4: rep Rnd 2.

Rnd 5: rep Rnd 1.

Rnd 6: MC.

Rnd 7: (MC, k1, CC, k3), rep to end.

Rnd 8: (MC, k1, CC, k1), rep to end.

Rnd 9: rep Rnd 7.

Rnd 10: rep Rnd 6.

Rep these 10 rnds once more.**

DIVIDE FOR THUMB

Keeping continuity of established patt:

Rnd 21: work 4 (4, 8) sts. With CC, k1fb next st, PM, continue in patt to end of rnd—65 (69, 73) sts.

Rnd 22: work 5 (5, 9) sts, PM. (With MC, kf, with CC, kb, with MC, kf) in same st, SM, continue in patt to end of rnd—67 (71, 75) sts.

Rnd 23: work 5 (5, 9) sts, SM. (With CC, kf, with MC, kb) in same st, with CC, k1. (With MC, kf, with CC, kb) in same st, SM, continue in patt to end of rnd—69 (73, 77) sts.

Rnd 24: work 5 (5, 9) sts, SM. (With MC, kf, with CC, kb) in same st, MC, k1, CC, k1, MC, k1. (With CC, kf, MC, kb) in same st, SM, continue in patt to end of rnd—71 (75, 79) sts.

Rnds 25–29: Continue working the thumb incs as established, making sure the colors line up, by using both colors in the k1fb st until there are 17 (19, 21) sts in the thumb—88 (94, 100) sts.

Rnd 30: work 5 (5, 9) sts, place sts between markers onto waste yarn or st holder, and continue in patt to end of rnd, being sure to check your tension between the 5th and 6th (5th and 6th, 9th and 10th) st.

Continue in patt until the body of the hand warmer is 1" shorter than final length.

Work 1" of cuff pattern and BO.

THUMB

With RS facing, pu and k17 (19, 21) sts from waste yarn or st holder, being sure to keep continuity of color patt as established. Pu and k5 (7, 9) sts across the gap, in alternate colors, and then k for 1 (1.5, 2)" or desired length. BO.

LEFT-HAND CUFF

Work in pattern as for Right-Hand Cuff from ** to **.

DIVIDE FOR THUMB

Keeping continuity of established patt:

Rnd 21: work 26 (26, 30) sts. With CC, k1fb next st, PM, continue in patt to end of rnd—65 (69, 73) sts.

Rnd 22: work 27 (27, 31) sts, PM. (With MC, kf, with CC, kb, with MC, kf) in same st, SM, then continue in patt to end of rnd—67 (71, 75) sts.

Rnd 23: work 27 (27, 31) sts, SM. (With CC, kf, with MC, kb) in same st, with CC, k1. (With MC, kf, with CC, kb) in same st, SM, continue in patt to end of rnd—69 (73, 77) sts.

Rnd 24: work 27 (27, 31) sts, SM. (With MC, kf, with CC, kb) in same st, MC, k1, CC, k1, MC, k1. (With CC, kf, MC, kb) in same st, SM, then continue in patt to end of rnd—71 (75, 79) sts.

Rnds 25–29: continue working the thumb incs as established, making sure the colors line up, by using both colors in the k1fb st until there are 17 (19, 21) in the thumb—88 (94, 100) sts.

Rnd 30: work 27 (27, 31) sts, place sts between markers onto waste yarn or st holder, and continue in patt to end of rnd, being sure to check your tension between the 27th and 28th (27th and 28th, 31st and 32nd) st.

Continue in patt until the body of the hand warmer is 1" shorter than final length.

Work 1" of cuff pattern and BO.

THUMB

With RS facing, pu and k17 (19, 21) sts from waste yarn or st holder, being sure to keep continuity of color patt as established. Pu and k5 (7, 9) sts across the gap, in alternate colors, and then k for 1 (1.5, 2)" or desired length. BO.

finishing

Turn the hand warmer inside out and, using the large-eyed blunt needle, weave in the ends, making sure to match colors.

dutch girl headscarf

BY SHANNON OKEY

Anyone who knows me knows that I frequently (read: about 99 percent of the time) wear bandannas or other headscarves to keep my hair out of my face. In fact, there are even photos of my mom and me wearing matching ones when I was about seven. I thought about dressing up an ordinary bandanna for cuter craftiness, and this was the result.

SIZE

One size, easily adjusted

FINISHED MEASUREMENTS

Dimensions: 20" around head;
    8" long sides of triangle

MATERIALS

Kollage Cornucopia (100% corn;
    100 yd per 34 g skein); color:
    Brandy; 1 skein

16" U.S. #8/5 mm circular needle

0.5 yard contrasting ribbon
    (see "Pattern Notes")

1 or more fancy buttons of your choice

Sewing thread to match the
    color of your ribbon

Sewing needle

Tapestry or yarn needle

Straight pins

GAUGE

Gauge is not critical to this pattern.

PATTERN NOTES

When choosing a ribbon for the edging, realize that its stiffness will play a part in how the edge is shaped and how the decorative flourish on the side stands up. If you choose a very stiff ribbon, as here, the flourish will stand up nicely but so will the edge of the headscarf. If you prefer a more laid-back look, you may want to choose a softer ribbon (such as velvet) for the edging and a different, stiff, contrasting one for the flourish.

directions

CO 80 sts and join rnd, being careful not to twist.

K 10 rnds or desired length of band (this will tuck behind your hair, so it should be at least 1"—you may make it thicker if you like).

K back and forth in St st, form the triangle as follows:

Row 1: sl first st and k across 50 sts, k2tog.

Row 2: sl first st and p back across, p2tog.

Rep rows 1 and 2 until 10 or less sts remain (less for a pointier tip), BO.

finishing

Weave in any yarn ends.

Pin ribbon for scarf edging around edge, folding it over the slipped-stitch edging of the scarf.

Sew ribbon into place with coordinating thread.

On one or both sides, loop ribbon against itself several times and sew into place.

Sew button(s) over ribbon loops.

de fleur socks

BY AMY GUMM

These socks feature a complex, twisted-cable stitch and corn yarn—the dense stitch makes the socks extremely comfortable, and the decorative minaret-style cable on the sides looks great with any kind of outfit. This is a true delight for sock knitters.

MATERIALS

Crystal Palace Yarns Maizy (82% corn fiber, 18% elastic nylon; 204 yds per 50 g skein); color: #1217 Nut Brown; 2 skeins

2 sets U.S. #1/2.25 mm circular or 1 set of 4 U.S. #1/2.25 mm double-pointed needles

1 small cable needle or spare U.S. #1/2.25 mm double-pointed needle

Tapestry needle

GAUGE

28 sts and 28 rows = 4" in stockinette stitch

PATTERN NOTES

Cable Panel (Center; worked in the rnd over 29 sts)

On the following page are the cable charts you will need for these socks. Actual cast-on directions begin after the charts.

Rnds 1–3: p11, k7 tbl, p11.

Rnd 4: p8, sl 3 to cn, hold in back, (k1 tbl, p1 from cn) 3 times, k1 tbl, sl 3 to cn, hold in front (p1, k1 tbl from cn) 3 times, p8.

Rnd 5: p8, (k1 tbl, p1) 6 times, k1 tbl, p8.

Rnd 6: p6, sl 2 to cn, hold in back, k1 tbl, p2 from cn, (p1, k1 tbl) 5 times, p1, sl 1 to cn, hold in front, p2, k1 tbl from cn, p6.

Rnd 7: p6, k1 tbl, p3, (k1 tbl, p1) 4 times, k1 tbl, p3, k1 tbl, p6.

Rnd 8: p4, sl 2 to cn, hold in back, k1 tbl, p2 from cn, p1, sl 2 to cn, hold in back, k1 tbl, p2 from cn, sl 1 to cn, hold in back, k1 tbl, p1 from cn, p1, k1 tbl, p1, sl 1 to cn, hold in front, p1, k1 tbl from cn, sl 1 to cn, hold in front, p2, k1 tbl from cn, p1, sl 1 to cn, hold in front, p2, k1 tbl from cn, p4.

Rnd 9: p4, k1 tbl, p3, (k1 tbl, p2) 4 times, k1 tbl, p3, k1 tbl, p4.

Rnd 10: p3, (sl 1 to cn, hold in back, k1 tbl, p1 from cn, p2) twice, (k1 tbl, p2) 3 times, sl 1 to cn, hold in front, p1, k1 tbl from cn, p2, sl 1 to cn, hold in front, p1, k1 tbl from cn, p3.

Rnd 11: (p3, k1 tbl) 3 times, (p2, k1 tbl) twice, (p3, k1 tbl) twice, p3.

Rnd 12: (p2, sl 1 to cn, hold in back, k1 tbl, p1 from cn) 3 times, p2, k1 tbl, (p2, sl 1 to cn, hold in front, p1, k1 tbl from cn) 3 times, p2.

Rnds 13–17: p2, (k1 tbl, p3) 6 times, k1 tbl, p2.

Rnd 18: (p2, sl 1 to cn, hold in front, p1, k1 tbl from cn) 3 times, p2, k1 tbl, (p2, sl 1 to cn, hold in back, k1 tbl, p1 from cn) 3 times, p2.

Rnd 19: (p3, k1 tbl) 3 times, (p2, k1 tbl) twice, (p3, k1 tbl) twice, p3.

Rnd 20: p3, (sl 1 to cn, hold in front, p1, k1 tbl from cn, p2) 2 times, (k1 tbl, p2) 3 times, sl 1 to cn, hold in back, k1 tbl, p1 from cn, p2, sl 1 to cn, hold in back, k1 tbl, p1 from cn, p3.

continued

Cable Panel (Center)

29 28 27 26 25 24 23 22 21 20 19 18 17 16 15 14 13 12 11 10 9 8 7 6 5 4 3 2 1

(chart grid, rows numbered 1, 3, 5, 7, 9, 11, 13, 15, 17, 19, 21, 23, 25, 27, 29)

Legend:

- ● Purl
- B Knit tbl
- C3 over 3 right P
- C3 over 3 left P
- C1 over 2 right P
- C1 over 2 left P
- C2 over 1 right P
- Right twist, purl background
- Left twist, purl background
- Right twist, purl background
- C2 over 4 left P
- C2 over 4 right P

Rnd 21: p4, k1 tbl, p3, (k1 tbl, p2) 4 times, k1 tbl, p3, k1 tbl, p4.

Rnd 22: p4, sl 1 to cn, hold in front, p2, k1 tbl from cn, p1, sl 1 to cn, hold in front, p2, k1 tbl from cn, sl 1 to cn, hold in front, p1, k1 tbl from cn, p1, k1 tbl, p1, sl 1 to cn, hold in back, k1 tbl, p1 from cn, sl 2 to cn, hold in back, k1 tbl, p2 from cn, p1, sl 2 to cn, hold in back, k1 tbl, p2 from cn, p4.

Rnd 23: p6, k1 tbl, p3, (k1 tbl, p1) 4 times, k1 tbl, p3, k1 tbl, p6.

Rnd 24: p6, sl 1 to cn, hold in front, p2, k1 tbl from cn, (p1, k1 tbl) 5 times, p1, sl 2 to cn, hold in back, k1 tbl, p2 from cn, p6.

Rnd 25: p8, (k1 tbl, p1) 6 times, k1 tbl, p8.

Rnd 26: p8, (sl 1 to cn, hold in front, p1) 3 times, k3 from cn tbl, k1 tbl, (sl 1 to cn and hold in back, k1 tbl) 3 times, p3 from cn, p8.

Rnds 27–30: p11, k7 tbl, p11.

Cable Panel (Left Foot)

Rnds 1–3: p11, k4 tbl.

Rnd 4: p8, sl 3 to cn, hold in back, (k1 tbl, p1 from cn) 3 times, k1 tbl.

Rnd 5: p8, (k1 tbl, p1) 6 times, k1 tbl, p8.

Rnd 6: p6, sl 2 to cn, hold in back, k1 tbl, p2 from cn, (p1, k1 tbl) 3 times.

Rnd 7: p6, k1 tbl, p3, (k1 tbl, p1) 2 times, k1 tbl.

Rnd 8: p4, sl 2 to cn, hold in back, k1 tbl, p2 from cn, p1, sl 2 to cn, hold in back, k1 tbl, p2 from cn, sl 1 to cn, hold in back, k1 tbl, p1 from cn, p1, k1 tbl.

Cable Panel (Left Foot)

15 14 13 12 11 10 9 8 7 6 5 4 3 2 1

(chart rows numbered 1, 3, 5, 7, 9, 11, 13, 15, 17, 19, 21, 23, 25, 27, 29)

Cable Panel (Right Foot)

15 14 13 12 11 10 9 8 7 6 5 4 3 2 1

(chart rows numbered 1, 3, 5, 7, 9, 11, 13, 15, 17, 19, 21, 23, 25, 27, 29)

Rnd 9: p4, k1 tbl, p3, (k1 tbl, p2) 2 times, k1 tbl.

Rnd 10: p3, (sl 1 to cn, hold in back, k1 tbl, p1 from cn, p2) twice, k1 tbl, p2, k1 tbl.

Rnd 11: (p3, k1 tbl) 3 times, p2, k1 tbl.

Rnd 12: (p2, sl 1 to cn, hold in back, k1 tbl, p1 from cn) 3 times, p2, k1 tbl.

Rnds 13–17: p2, (k1 tbl, p3) 3 times, k1 tbl.

Rnd 18: (p2, sl 1 to cn, hold in front, p1, k1 tbl from cn) 3 times, p2, k1 tbl.

Rnd 19: (p3, k1 tbl) 3 times, p2, k1 tbl.

Rnd 20: p3, (sl 1 to cn, hold in front, p1, k1 tbl from cn, p2) 2 times, k1 tbl, p2, k1 tbl.

Rnd 21: p4, k1 tbl, p3, (k1 tbl, p2) 2 times, k1 tbl.

Rnd 22: p4, sl 1 to cn, hold in front, p2, k1 tbl from cn, p1, sl 1 to cn, hold in front, p2, k1 tbl from cn, sl 1 to cn, hold in front, p1, k1 tbl from cn, p1, k1 tbl.

Rnd 23: p6, k1 tbl, p3, (k1 tbl, p1) 2 times, k1 tbl.

Rnd 24: p6, sl 1 to cn, hold in front, p2, k1 tbl from cn, (p1, k1 tbl) 3 times.

Rnd 25: p8, (k1 tbl, p1) 3 times, k1 tbl.

Rnd 26: p8, (sl 1 to cn, hold in front, p1) 3 times, k3 from cn tbl, k1 tbl.

Rnds 27–30: p11, k4 tbl.

Cable Panel (Right Foot)

Rnds 1–3: k4 tbl, p11.

Rnd 4: k1 tbl, sl 3 to cn, hold in front (p1, k1 tbl from cn) 3 times, p8.

Rnd 5: (k1 tbl, p1) 3 times, k1 tbl, p8.

Rnd 6: (k1 tbl, p1) 3 times, sl 1 to cn, hold in front, p2, k1 tbl from cn, p6.

Rnd 7: (k1 tbl, p1) 2 times, k1 tbl, p3, k1 tbl, p6.

Rnd 8: k1 tbl, p1, sl 1 to cn, hold in front, p1, k1 tbl from cn, sl 1 to cn, hold in front, p2, k1 tbl from cn, p1, sl 1 to cn, hold in front, p2, k1 tbl from cn, p4.

Rnd 9: (k1 tbl, p2) 2 times, k1 tbl, p3, k1 tbl, p4.

continued

Rnd 10: (k1 tbl, p2) 2 times, sl 1 to cn, hold in front, p1, k1 tbl from cn, p2, sl 1 to cn, hold in front, p1, k1 tbl from cn, p3.

Rnd 11: k1 tbl, p2, (k1 tbl, p3) 3 times.

Rnd 12: k1 tbl, (p2, sl 1 to cn, hold in front, p1, k1 tbl from cn) 3 times, p2.

Rnds 13–17: (k1 tbl, p3) 3 times, k1 tbl, p2.

Rnd 18: k1 tbl, (p2, sl 1 to cn, hold in back, k1 tbl, p1 from cn) 3 times, p2.

Rnd 19: k1 tbl, p2, (k1 tbl, p3) 3 times.

Rnd 20: (k1 tbl, p2) 2 times, sl 1 to cn, hold in back, k1 tbl, p1 from cn, p2, sl 1 to cn, hold in back, k1 tbl, p1 from cn, p3.

Rnd 21: (k1 tbl, p2) 2 times, k1 tbl, p3, k1 tbl, p4.

Rnd 22: k1 tbl, p1, sl 1 to cn, hold in back, k1 tbl, p1 from cn, sl 2 to cn, hold in back, k1 tbl, p2 from cn, p1, sl 2 to cn, hold in back, k1 tbl, p2 from cn, p4.

Rnd 23: (k1 tbl, p1) 2 times, k1 tbl, p3, k1 tbl, p6.

Rnd 24: (k1 tbl, p1) 3 times, sl 2 to cn, hold in back, k1 tbl, p2 from cn, p6.

Rnd 25: (k1 tbl, p1) 3 times, k1 tbl, p8.

Rnd 26: k1 tbl, (sl 1 to cn and hold in back, k1 tbl) 3 times, p3 from cn, p8.

Rnds 27–30: k4 tbl, p11.

directions

CUFF

CO 72 sts. Divide stitches evenly between needles and join to begin working in the round, being careful not to twist.

Rnd 1: (k1 tbl, p1) to end.

Rep this rnd 14 more times (15 rows total).

LEFT LEG

Setup Rnd/Rnd1: k21, pm, p11, k7 tbl, p11, pm, k22.

Rnd 2: k to marker, work Rnd 2 of cable pattern, k to end of rnd.

Cont in this manner, k to first marker, working cable pattern, and k to the end of the rnd.

Work cable pattern in this manner twice, stopping after Row 27 when working the second rep.

RIGHT LEG

Setup Rnd/Rnd 1: k21, pm, p11, k7 tbl, p11, pm, k22.

Rnd 2: k to marker, work Rnd 2 of cable pattern, k to end of rnd.

Cont in this manner, k to first marker, working cable pattern, and k to the end of the rnd.

Work cable pattern in this manner twice, stopping after Row 26 when working the second rep.

HEEL FLAP

Row 1: (sl 1, k1) to end.

Row 2: sl 1 pwise, p to end.

Rep these two rows 16 times more (17 times total).

TURN HEEL

Row 1: sl 1, k17, ssk, k1. Turn.

Row 2: sl 1, p5, p2tog, p1. Turn.

Row 3: sl 1, k6, ssk, k1. Turn.

Row 4: sl 1, p7, p2tog, p1. Turn.

Row 5: sl 1, k8, ssk, k1. Turn.

Row 6: sl 1, p9, p2tog, p1. Turn.

Row 7: sl 1, k10, ssk, k1. Turn.

Row 8: sl 1, p11, p2tog, p1. Turn.

Row 9: sl 1, k12, ssk, k1. Turn.

Row 10: sl 1, p13, p2tog, p1. Turn.

Row 11: sl 1, k14, ssk, k1. Turn.

Row 12: sl 1, p15, p2tog, p1. Turn.

Row 13: sl 1, k16, ssk, k1. Turn.

Row 14: sl 1, p17, p2tog, p1. Turn.

Row 15: sl 1, k18, ssk, k1. Turn.

Row 16: sl 1, p19, p2tog, p1. Turn.

Row 17: sl 1, k20, ssk, k1. Turn.

Row 18: sl 1, p21, p2tog, p1. Turn

LEFT SOCK GUSSET

Next Rnd: k across all heel sts. Pu and k18 sts along heel flap. Work instep sts as foll: k21, work Row 28 of left cable pattern. With spare DPN, pu and k18 sts along heel flap.

Next Rnd: k to last 3 sts before instep, k2tog, k1. K21, work next row of left cable pattern. K1, ssk, k remaining sts on spare DPN.

Next Rnd: k across to instep, k21, work next row of left cable pattern, k across all sts on spare DPN.

Rep previous 2 rnds until 36 heel sts rem. Redistribute heel sts among DPNs or circular needles.

RIGHT SOCK GUSSET

Next Rnd: k across all heel sts. Pu and k18 sts along heel flap. Work instep sts as foll: Work Row 27 of right cable pattern, k21. With spare DPN, pu and k18 sts along heel flap.

Next Rnd: knit to last 3 sts before instep, k2tog, k1. K21, work next row of right cable pattern. K1, ssk, k rem sts on spare DPN.

Next Rnd: k across to instep, k21, work next row of right cable pattern, k across all sts on spare DPN.

Rep previous 2 rounds until 36 heel sts rem. Redistribute heel sts among DPNs or circular needles.

LEFT FOOT

Cont left cable pattern on instep sts and k all sts on remainder of foot. Rep the cable pattern twice. To reach desired length, rep Rnd 1 of left cable pattern on the instep until approx 1" from the toe decs.

Next Instep Row: k22, p10, k4 tbl.

Next Instep Row: k23, p9, k4 tbl.

Next Instep Row: k24, p8, k4 tbl.

Next Instep Row: k25, p7, k4 tbl.

Next Instep Row: k26, p6, k4 tbl.

Next Instep Row: k27, p5, k4 tbl.

Next Instep Row: k28, p4, k4 tbl.

Next Instep Row: k29, p3, k4 tbl.

Next Instep Row: k30, p2, k4 tbl.

Next Instep Row: k31, p1, k4 tbl.

RIGHT FOOT

Cont right cable pattern on instep sts and k all sts on remainder of foot. Rep the cable pattern twice. To reach desired length, rep Rnd 1 of right cable pattern on the instep until approx 1" from the toe decs.

Next Instep Row: k4 tbl, p10, k22.

Next Instep Row: k4 tbl, p9, k23.

Next Instep Row: k4 tbl, p8, k24.

Next Instep Row: k4 tbl, p7, k25.

Next Instep Row: k4 tbl, p6, k26.

Next Instep Row: k4 tbl, p5, k27.

Next Instep Row: k4 tbl, p4, k28.

Next Instep Row: k4 tbl, p3, k29.

Next Instep Row: k4 tbl, p2, k30.

Next Instep Row: k4 tbl, p1, k31.

TOE

Rnd 1: k1, ssk, k to last 3 sts, k2tog, k1

Rnd 2: work all sts.

Rep these 2 rounds until 16 sts rem on each needle. Graft rem sts using Kitchener stitch.

finishing

Weave in ends. Block socks in lukewarm water and lay flat to dry. Do not iron the socks, as Crystal Palace Maizy contains fibers that will melt with an iron.

sunny-side-up socks

BY ANDI SMITH

This toe-up, patterned sock features a four-stitch twisted rib and simple lace to create a wonderfully stretchy fabric that will skim pleasingly over your leg curves yet requires less shaping than a stockinette knee sock.

SIZE

This is a very stretchy sock and will fit most legs with ease.

FINISHED MEASUREMENTS

Unstretched: 8" wide across the foot, 9.5" wide across the calf, 14" long from the cuff to the bottom of the heel.

MATERIALS

Crystal Palace Yarn Panda Cotton (55% bamboo, 24% cotton, 21% elastic nylon; 182 yd per 50 g); color: #3646 Yellow; 4 skeins

2 sets 24" U.S. #1/2.5 mm circular needles

3 yards smooth waste yarn

Large-eyed, blunt needle

GAUGE

36 sts and 36 rows = 4" in lace pattern unstretched

YARN NOTES

Because this yarn contains elastic, it's important not to stretch it too much as you are knitting, but to find a comfortable tension. Working a gauge swatch will help you correct your tension. Like many yarns that are made up of multiple fibers, Panda Cotton has a tendency to be a little splitty. Using metal needles and completely finishing each stitch before moving on to the next one greatly reduces splitting.

SPECIAL ABBREVIATIONS

TW2: knit 2 together, but do not take the sts off the left-hand needle, knit through the front loop of the first stitch, then take both sts off the left-hand needle.

directions

Using your preferred method, provisionally CO 12 sts with waste yarn.

Row 1: knit.

Row 2: purl.

Carefully pull out the provisional CO and k through back loop of the 12 live sts onto your second needle. You are now working with both circular needles and in the round—24 sts.

Rnd 1: k1, m1, k to last 2 sts of needle, m1, k1; rep for second needle—28 sts.

Rep Rnd 1, 9 more times—64 sts.

Rearrange your sts so that you have 31 on the front needle and 33 on the back needle.

With lace pattern on the front needle and St st on the back needle, work the foot as follows:

Rnd 1: Needle 1—(TW2, yo, k2tog tbl, k1, k2tog, yo) to last 4 sts, end with TW2. Needle 2—k.

Lace Pattern

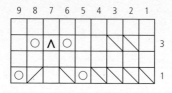

9	8	7	6	5	4	3	2	1	
	○	∧	○						3
○	/			○	/		/		1

○	Yo	◹	K2tog
◺	Ssk	∧	K3tog
	Knit	◺◹	Left twist

Rnd 2: knit.

Rnd 3: Needle 1—(k1, TW2, k2, yo, sl1pw, k2tog, psso, yo, k1) to last 4 sts, k1, TW2, k1. Needle 2—k.

Rnd 4: knit.

Rep these 4 rnds until foot measures 2" short of total foot measurement. Dec 1 st at the end of the second needle on the last rnd—63 sts total.

HEEL

Row 1: k31, wrap and turn.

Row 2: p across to the last st, wrap and turn.

Row 3: k across to the st before the unworked st, wrap and turn.

Row 4: p across to the st before the unworked st, wrap and turn.

Cont rows 3 and 4 until 14 sts are left in the middle, and there are 9 wrapped sts on each side ending on a RS row.

For the second part of the heel:

Row 1: k across 14 sts to the first wrapped st. Pu the wrap and k it tog with the st. Wrap and turn the next st (it now has 2 wraps).

Row 2: sl that st and p across to the first wrapped st. Pu the wrap and p it tog with the st. Wrap and turn the next st (it now has 2 wraps).

Cont rows 1 and 2, pu both wraps, and k or p them tog with the st until you have 32 unwrapped sts.

With RS facing, and working on both needles, beg with front of sock, work in patt across both needles for about 3".

Cont working the first needle in established patt, and work the following inc on the second needle only:

Rnd 1: k1, yo, sl1, k2tog, psso, yo, k1, k1fb, TW2, k1fb, k1, yo, sl1, k2tog, psso, yo, k2, TW2, k2, yo, sl1, k2tog, psso, yo, k1, k1fb, TW2, k1fb, k1, yo, sl1, k2tog, psso, yo, k1—31 sts on needle 1; 36 sts on needle 2.

Rnd 2 (and all even rnds): knit.

Rnd 3: yo, ssk, k1, k2tog, yo, k1fb, TW2, TW2, k1fb, yo, ssk, k1, k2tog, yo, k1, TW2, k1, yo, ssk, k1, k2tog, yo, k1fb, TW2, TW2, k1fb, yo, ssk, k1, k2tog, yo—40 sts on needle 2.

Rnd 5: k1, yo, sl1, k2tog, psso, yo, k2, TW2, k1, yo, k1, TW2, k2, yo, sl1, k2tog, psso, yo, k2, TW2, k2, yo, sl1, k2tog, psso, yo, k2, TW2, k1, yo, k1, TW2, k2, yo, sl1, k2tog, psso, yo, k1—42 sts on needle 2.

Rnd 7: yo, ssk, k1, k2tog, yo, TW2, TW2, yo, k1, yo TW2, TW2, yo, ssk, k1, k2tog, yo, TW2, TW2, yo, ssk, k1, k2tog, yo, TW2, TW2, yo, k1, yo, TW2, TW2, yo, ssk, k1, k2tog, yo—46 sts on needle 2.

Rnd 9: k1, yo, sl1, k2tog, psso, yo, k2, TW2, k2, yo, k1, yo, k2, TW2, k2, yo, sl1, k2tog, psso, yo, k2, TW2, k2, yo, sl1, k2tog, psso, yo, k2, TW2, k2, yo, k1, yo, k2, TW2, k2, yo, sl1, k2tog, psso, yo, k1—50 sts on needle 2.

Cont working lace pattern until leg measures 2" shorter than desired length.

CUFF

Rnd 1: *k1tbl, p1, rep from * to end.

Rep Rnd 1 for 2".

To BO: Place all the k sts on one needle and the p sts on another needle. Holding both needles tog, use Kitchener stitch to BO.

zenluv socks

BY ANDI SMITH

Named after a band Andi loved in the '80s, this sock highlights the richness of the yarn with a heavily cabled, yet simple pattern. This sock looks great as both an ankle sock and a midcalf sock.

SIZE

S (M, L)

(It is shown here in size medium.)

FINISHED MEASUREMENTS

Dimensions: 7 (8, 9)" across the instep unstretched; 8.5 (9.5, 10.5)" stretched.

MATERIALS

Crystal Palace Yarn Panda Cotton (55% bamboo, 24% cotton, 21% elastic nylon; 182 yd per 50 g), color: #0204 Ivory; 3 skeins

2 sets 24" U.S. #1/2.5 mm circular needles

Large-eyed, blunt needle

GAUGE

40 sts and 40 rows = 4" in cable pattern unstretched

YARN NOTES

Because this yarn contains elastic, it's important not to stretch it too much as you are knitting, but to find a comfortable tension. Working a gauge swatch will help you correct your tension. Like many yarns that are made up of multiple fibers, Panda Cotton has a tendency to be a little splitty. Using metal needles and completely finishing each stitch before moving on to the next one greatly reduces splitting.

SPECIAL ABBREVIATIONS

C4L: slip 2 stitches onto cable needle and hold at the front of your work, knit the next 2 stitches, then the 2 stitches from the cable needle.

C4R: slip 2 stitches onto cable needle and hold at the back of your work, knit the next 2 stitches, then the 2 stitches from the cable needle.

directions

CUFF

Using German twisted, or your preferred stretchy CO method, CO 60 (70, 80) sts.

Divide the sts so there are 30 (35, 40) sts on each needle.

Being careful not to twist your work, p 2 rnds.

Foundation Rnd 1: p1, k4, *p1, k4; rep from * to end.

Rnd 2: p1, C4L, *p1, C4R, p1, C4L; rep from * to end.

Rnd 3: p1, k4, *p1, k4; rep from * to end.

Rnd 4: as Rnd 2.

Rnd 5: p1, C4R, *p1, C4L, p1, C4R; rep from * to end.

Rnd 6: as Rnd 2.

Rnd 7: as Rnd 2.

Cable Pattern

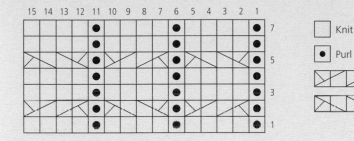

	Knit
●	Purl
C2 over 2 left
C2 over 2 right

Rep rnds 2–7 until the sock measures desired length for leg, ending after Rnd 4 or Rnd 7.

HEEL

Turn. Working on second needle only:

Row 1 (WS): sl 1, p to end, turn.

For M size only: p2tog at end of needle—30 (34, 40) sts.

Row 2 (RS): *sl 1, k1tbl; rep from * to end, turn.

Rep these 2 rows 15 (17, 19) times, then rep Row 1 once.

HEEL TURN

Row 1 (RS): sl 1, k19 (21, 23) sts, ssk, turn.

Row 2 (WS): sl 1pw, p10 (10, 10) sts, p2tog, turn.

Row 3: sl 1, k10, ssk, turn.

Row 4: sl 1pw, p10, p2tog, turn.

Rep rows 1 and 2 until all sts are incorporated—12 (12, 12) sts.

GUSSET

With RS facing, and working on both needles, pu and k16 (18, 20) sts along left heel flap, work patt across first needle, then pu 16 (18, 20) sts along right heel flap and k to end of second needle—35 (40, 45) sts on first needle; 44 (48, 52) sts on second needle.

Working in patt across first needle (front of sock) throughout and the foll decs across second needle throughout (back of sock):

Rnd 1: k1, ssk, k to last 3 sts, k2tog, k1—42 (46, 50) sts on second needle.

Rnd 2: knit.

Rnd 3: knit.

Rep rnds 1–3, until you have 30 (34, 40) sts, then cont without shaping until the foot measures 2" shorter than desired length.

SHAPE TOES

Rnd 1: k1, ssk, k to 3 sts before end of needle, k2tog, k1; rep on second needle.

Rnd 2: knit.

Rep rnds 1 and 2 until you have 14 (16, 18) sts on each needle.

BO using Kitchener stitch or your preferred method.

finishing

Turn the sock inside out and weave in all ends. There is no need to block this sock—it's immediately wearable!

clever socks

BY EMMA JANE HOGBIN

The Clever Socks are so named because Emma Jane needed a placeholder name while she wrote the pattern. She never thought a variation on "clever name" would stick! These socks are basic but not at all boring, especially when worked in a charming multicolored yarn.

SIZE

One size fits women's feet, sizes 7–9.

FINISHED MEASUREMENTS

Dimensions: variable; pattern adjusts to be as tall and as long as you need.

MATERIALS

Fleece Artist Silk Cotton (50% silk, 50% cotton; 225 m per 100 g skein); color: (see "Yarn Notes"); 2 skeins

U.S. #2/2.75 mm double-pointed needles

Tapestry needle

GAUGE

24 sts and 26 rows = 4" in stockinette stitch

SPECIAL ABBREVIATIONS

C4B: cable 4 to back (2 over 2, with stitches held to back).

YARN NOTES

This is a lovely, soft yarn to work with. The addition of silk should add a bit of strength to the yarn—a highly valuable quality in sock yarn. This sock is knit as densely as possible to improve the wear of the sock. It does not have a lot of give, and so it is not ideal for those of you with a high arch. Either try one of the other patterns instead or choose a yarn with much more stretch, such as an elasticized cotton or bamboo (Panda Cotton, for example, or Cascade Fixation). This yarn is hand dyed by Fleece Artist. As they say on their website, "No two skeins are ever exactly alike; because of this we do not print color names on our labels." If you can't find two skeins that are very similar, alternate two "close enough" ones every few rows.

directions

CO 66 sts *loosely*.

LEG

Rnds 1–17: (k4, p2) to end.

Rnd 18: (C4B, p2) to end.

Rnds 19–26: (k4 p2) to end.

Rep rnds 18–26, 4 more times (total of 5 twists) or until leg reaches desired length, ending with Rnd 26.

HEEL FLAP

The heel flap uses 36 sts starting with 2 p sts. Count 34 sts from the beg of the row for the heel flap. Add to this the *last* 2 sts from the same rnd (they will be p sts located on the third needle). The first row of the heel flap is an extra set of cable twists. This will make your heel flap more snuggly.

Row 1: sl 1, p1, (C4B, p2) to end.

Row 2: sl 1, k1, p4, (k2, p4) to last 2 sts, k2.

Row 3: sl 1, k1, (k4, p2) to last 2 sts, k2.

Rep rows 2–3, 30 times (or until the heel flap is a square—you may need to tug a bit on the edges, as the garter st ridge gets a little stiff).

TURN HEEL

Row 1: sl 1, k15, s1, k1, psso, k1. Turn work.

Row 2: p6, p2tog, p1. Turn work.

Row 3: k to 1 st before the gap. Sl 1, k1, psso, k1. Turn work.

Row 4: p to 1 st before the gap. P2tog, p1. Turn work.

Rep rows 3–4 until you reach the edge of the heel flap on both sides.

When you turn the work for the last time, you should be looking at the *outside* of the sock. If you are looking at the inside (p side), p 1 row, turn work.

GUSSET

Rnd 1: K across the heel flap. Pu 1 st for each garter st ridge along the heel flap. K across these picked-up sts.

Cont along the second needle in rib pattern (k4, p2). Using your third needle, pu 1 st for each garter st ridge along the next heel flap edge. K across these sts.

Count the number of sts on the first and third needles. Divide this number in half. Determine how many sts you need to move from needle 1 to needle 3 so they have the same number of sts. K this number of sts and sl them onto the third (last) needle. The middle-bottom of the foot is now the beg of your row.

Rnd 2: K to the last 3 sts on the needle, k2tog, k1.

Cont rib patt across the second needle (k4, p2), k1, sl 1, psso.

K to end.

Rnd 3: K sts on first needle, cont rib pattern on second needle, k sts on third needle.

Rep rnds 2–3 until total sts rem is 66 (original number sts CO).

FOOT

Cont in patt until work measures desired foot length, less 1.5" from bottom of heel flap (back of foot).

TOE

Edward "Ted" Myatt, known online as "The Knitter Guy," taught me this toe. Ted knits intricate lace shawls but does not enjoy Kitchener stitch. Welcome to the dark side. Your toes will never be the same.

Count the number of sts currently on needle 1. Divide this number by 2. This becomes your Magic Number.

Rnd 1: knit.

Rnd 2: k to last 3 sts on needle 1, k2tog, k1;

Needle 2: k1, sl 1, psso, k to last 3 sts on needle, k2tog, k1;

Needle 3: k1, sl 1, psso, k to end of needle.

Rep rnds 1–2 until the number of sts rem on needle 1 is the Magic Number (half of the original number of sts).

Dec every rnd using the shaping established in Rnd 2 of toe instructions.

Cont until 4 sts remain. Cut yarn and draw through the last 4 sts. Do not try to break this wool-silk yarn. It is stronger than you are. Trust me.

finishing

Weave in ends.

Second sock. Rep instructions as for the first sock but reverse the cable pattern on the leg by pulling the cable needle to the front (C4F) instead of to the back as for the first foot. Socks are interchangeable and not limited to either the left or right foot.

kenaf spike-stitch bag

BY JULIE ARMSTRONG HOLETZ

I asked *Uncommon Crochet* author and friend Julie Armstrong Holetz if she could replicate an African-style spherical bag with leather straps she owned using crochet. The answer? Of course! This is a tough bag, suitable for just about anything you can throw at it (or in it, for that matter), and attractive, too. Grab yourself a crochet hook and have fun!

FINISHED MEASUREMENTS

Dimensions: 15.5" wide (at top) x 14" high

MATERIALS

Main color (MC): Habu Textiles Kenaf XS-19 (100% kenaf; 167 yd per 28 g; lace weight); color: Natural; 1 skein wound into 2 balls

Contrasting color (CC). 2 mm jute twine, 2 ply (100% jute; 100 yd per 0.3 lb); color: #6 Brown

U.S. #9/I/5.5 mm crochet hook

Stitch marker

Yarn needle

1 pair 20" brown sew-on leather straps (shown in Homestead Heirlooms LLC dark brown; comes with waxed linen and 8 buttons)

Waxed linen for sewing strap

8 1" wood buttons

12 assorted beads

Sewing needle and thread to match bag

GAUGE

14 sts and 18 rows = 4" in single crochet

PATTERN NOTES

Main color is worked double-stranded throughout; contrast color uses only a single strand.

The pattern is worked in joined rounds, turning at the end of each round. After turning, skip the slip stitch and begin the round in the first stitch following the slip stitch, which will create an almost invisible seam.

The turning chain does not count as a stitch.

Herringbone half double crochet (hhdc):

Yo, insert hook in st, yo and pull up a loop (3 loops on hook), do not yo, draw first loop on hook through second loop on hook (2 loops on hook), yo and draw through both loops on hook.

Double crochet spike stitch (sp5-dc):

Yo, insert hook into st 5 rnds below next st on previous rnd, yo and pull up a long loop to the height of the working rnd, (yo and draw through 2 loops on hook) twice.

Adjustable ring:

Leaving 6" of tail, wrap the yarn around two fingers with the working yarn laying across the tail end of the yarn to make a ring, insert the hook into the ring and pull up a loop of the working yarn as if to make a slip knot but do not tighten the loop around the hook. Ch 1, then begin working the foundation rnd of sts into the large ring. Once the foundation rnd of sts is complete, pull the tail end to close the ring.

continued

Spike Stitch Pattern (sp st patt)

Rnd 1 (WS): ch 1, sk sl st, sc in each st around, sl st in first sc to join, turn.

Rnd 2: ch 1, sk sl st, sc in each st around, changing to CC with last st, sl st in first sc, turn.

Rnd 3: ch 1, sk sl st, sc in each st around, changing to MC with last st, sl st in first sc, turn.

Rnd 4: rep Rnd 1.

Rnd 5: ch 1, sk sl st, hhdc in each st around, sl st in first sc, turn.

Rnd 6: rep Rnd 2.

Rnd 7: rep Rnd 3.

Rnds 8–9: rep Rnd 1.

Rnd 10: rep Rnd 2.

Rnd 11: ch 2, sk sl st, dc in each st around, changing to MC with last st, sl st in first dc, turn.

Rnds 12–14: rep Rnd 1.

Rnd 15: rep Rnd 2.

Rnd 16: ch 2, sk sl st, dc in each of next 3 sc, *sp5-dc, sk next sc on previous rnd, dc in each of next 5 sc; rep from * around, ending dc in each of last 2 sc and changing to MC with last st, sl st in first dc, turn.

Rep rnds 1–16 for pattern.

YARN NOTES

Kenaf comes from the hibiscus plant and is similar in nature to jute fibers. Despite its soft drape, Habu Kenaf XS-19 is inelastic and a little rough and textured, which gives it enough structure to be ideal for bags. In order to give it the same density as the 2-ply jute twine, hold the kenaf yarn doubled throughout.

directions

Rnd 1 (RS): using two strands of MC, make an adjustable ring and work 6 sc into ring, sl st in first sc, turn—6 sc.

Rnd 2: ch 1, sk sl st, 2 sc in each sc around, sl st in first sc, turn—12 sc.

Rnd 3: ch 1, sk sl st, *sc in next sc, 2 sc in next sc; rep from * around, sl st in first sc, turn—18 sc.

Rnd 4: ch 1, sk sl st, *2 sc in next sc, sc in each of next 2 sc; rep from * around, sl st in first sc, turn—24 sc.

Rnd 5: ch 1, sk sl st, *sc in each of next 3 sc, 2 sc in next sc; rep from * around, sl st in first sc, turn—30 sc.

Rnd 6: ch 1, sk sl st, *2 sc in next sc, sc in each of next 4 sc; rep from * around, sl st in first sc, turn—36 sc.

Rnd 7: ch 1, sk sl st, *sc in each of next 5 sc, 2 sc in next sc; rep from * around, sl st in first sc, turn—42 sc.

Rnd 8: ch 1, sk sl st, *2 sc in next sc, sc in each of next 6 sc; rep from * around, sl st in first sc, turn—48 sc.

Rnd 9: ch 1, sk sl st, *sc in each of next 7 sc, 2 sc in next sc; rep from * around, sl st in first sc, turn—54 sc.

Rnd 10: ch 1, sk sl st, *2 sc in next sc, sc in each of next 8 sc; rep from * around, sl st in first sc, turn—60 sc.

Rnd 11: ch 1, sk sl st, *sc in each of next 9 sc, 2 sc in next sc; rep from * around, sl st in first sc, turn—66 sc.

Rnd 12: ch 1, sk sl st, *2 sc in next sc, sc in each of next 10 sc; rep from * around, sl st in first sc, turn—72 sc.

Rnd 13: ch 1, sk sl st, *sc in each of next 11 sc, 2 sc in next sc; rep from * around, sl st in first sc, turn—78 sc.

Rnd 14: ch 1, sk sl st, *2 sc in next sc, sc in each of next 12 sc; rep from * around, sl st in first sc, turn—84 sc.

Rnd 15: ch 1, sk sl st, *sc in each of next 13 sc, 2 sc in next sc; rep from * around, sl st in first sc, turn—90 sc.

Rnd 16: ch 1, sk sl st, sc in each st around, sl st in first sc, turn.

Rnd 17: ch 1, sk sl st, *2 sc in next sc, sc in each of next 14 sc; rep from * around, sl st in first sc, turn—96 sc.

Rnd 18: ch 1, sk sl st, sc in each st around, sl st in first sc, turn.

Rnd 19: ch 1, sk sl st, *sc in each of next 23 sc, 2 sc in next sc; rep from * around, sl st in first sc, turn—100 sc.

Rnd 20: ch 1, sk sl st, sc in each st around, sl st in first sc, turn.

Rnd 21: ch 1, sk sl st, *2 sc in next sc, sc in each of next 24 sc; rep from * around, sl st in first sc, turn—104 sc.

Rnds 22–23: ch 1, sk sl st, sc in each st around, sl st in first sc, turn.

Rnd 24: ch 1, sk sl st, *sc in each of next 25 sc, 2 sc in next sc; rep from * around, sl st in first sc, turn—108 sc.

Work sp st patt 2 times marking Rnd 21 of patt rep for bead placement later, work rnds 1–7 of sp st patt once more. Fasten off and weave in ends.

finishing

With RS facing and using sewing needle and thread, sew beads evenly across the marked rnd on the front side of the bag.

Using waxed linen and yarn needle, sew one strap with buttons to each of the front and back, placing the edge of the strap 2" in from each side of the bag.

fuji table set

BY JILLIAN MORENO

Your table will appreciate the time you take to dress it with care! This set, consisting of a runner, place mats, napkins, and unique candle holders, will make sure it's dressed in style. Designer Jillian Moreno has pushed alt fibers to the edge with this set, but remarkably, it's also quite practical and hard wearing. You'll need basic crochet skills for these patterns, too, but they're well worth the effort!

FINISHED MEASUREMENTS

Runner: 14" x 90"

Place mats: 13" x 19"

Napkins: 16" x 16"

Candle Holders: fits around a regular Mason-style jar

MATERIALS

Runner

Habu Shosenshi Paper (100% linen; 560 yd per 1 oz skein); color: Purple; 1 skein

Habu Paper Moire (50% linen, 50% nylon; 311 yd per 1 oz skein); color: Brown; 1 skein

U.S. #7/4.5 mm straight needles

Place mats

Habu NIS-1 Handspun Nettle (100% nettle; skein yardage varies); color: Natural; 1 typical skein makes 2 place mats

U.S. #3/3.25 mm straight needles

Napkins

Habu Gear Linen (100% linen; 140 yd per 1 oz skein); color: Natural; 1 skein

Habu Bamboo (100% Bamboo; 167 yd per 1 oz skein); color: Natural; 4 skeins used double throughout

U.S. #10/6 mm straight needles

U.S. #10/J/6 mm or #10.5/K/6.5 mm crochet hook

Candle Holders

Main color (MC): Habu Handspun Hemp (100% hemp; yardage varies per skein); color: Natural; 1 bundle

Contrasting color (CC): Habu Hemp Bark (100% hemp; yardage varies per skein); color: Natural; 1 skein

U.S. #3/3 mm double-pointed needles

2 wide-mouthed Mason jars

GAUGE

Runner: 14 sts and 20 rows = 4" in stockinette stitch

Place mats: 16 sts and 22 rows = 4" in stockinette stitch

Napkins: 14 sts and 18 rows = 4" in stockinette stitch

Candle Holders: 14 sts and 17 rows = 4" in stockinette stitch

PATTERN NOTES

Runner: Hold both yarns together.

Napkins: Linen and two strands of bamboo are held together. These aren't the softest napkins you'll own, but the linen is fantastically cool!

Candle Holders: Dropped stitches are used to create the run of open stitches into which you'll weave the hemp bark strips. It's easy to do and very decorative.

runner directions
(make one)

CO 50 sts. Work 6 rows in garter stitch. Keeping first and last 5 sts in garter, work in St st for 89". Work 6 rows in garter stitch, BO loosely.

finishing

Mist block—do not immerse in water; just spray lightly with a spray bottle and lay flat to dry.

place mat directions (make two)

CO 60 sts.

Set up row: k10, p10, k10, p10, k10, p10.

Work sts as presented for 19".

BO loosely.

napkin directions
(make two)

CO 56 sts.

Work in St st for 16", then BO loosely.

Single crochet around the edge.

finishing

Wet block with hot water by immersing the pieces and then placing them flat to dry.

candle holder directions (make two)

With MC, CO 41 sts as follows: k on 5, yo, to last 5 sts, k on 5.

Join rnd.

Rnds 1–4: knit.

Rnd 5: k5, drop next st on needles, yo, rep to last 5 sts, k5.

Rep rnds 1–5 for 6". BO.

Manipulate knitting (i.e., stretch and poke dropped sts to form run of open sts).

Cut CC in 8" lengths.

Weave CC through dropped sts, and trim to desired look.

finishing

Slip knitting over Mason jars.

irish rose bolster

BY AMY O'NEILL HOUCK AND SHANNON OKEY

Using a traditional Irish Rose crochet motif, some 1930s-style colors, and knitting in the round or flat (your choice), you too can craft this gorgeous bolster pillow that will look stunning on your bed, couch, or anywhere else you need a little glam.

SIZE

Varies according to the size of the Irish Rose motif you crochet and your choice of length.

FINISHED MEASUREMENTS

Dimensions (as shown here): 7" diameter ends and 12" long; however, size is easily varied (see pattern).

MATERIALS

Blue Sky Alpacas Dyed Cotton (100% organically grown cotton; 157 yd/ 137 m per 100 g skein); main color (MC): #629 Ladybug, 1–2 skeins; contrasting color (CC): #627 Flamingo, 1 skein

16" U.S. #9/6 mm straight needles or circular needle (see "Pattern Notes")

U.S. #10/J/6 mm crochet hook

Bolster pillow form, available at sewing supply stores

0.5 yard coordinating cotton fabric

Coordinating sewing thread

Sewing needle

Yarn or tapestry needle

GAUGE

Gauge is not critical as long as the fabric is solid enough to hide the bolster underneath. Aim for approx 4 sts per inch.

PATTERN NOTES

This pillow can be knit in the round or flat. If you don't like to purl, go for knitting in the round. Directions for both follow.

The ends of this bolster are based on a traditional Irish Rose motif. The layers of petals are created by working crochet stitches into the back (wrong side) of stitches from the previous round. You do this by inserting the hook into any loop on the back of the indicated stitch and working a single crochet. These stitches won't be seen since the flower is sewn into the bolster, but the wrong side ends up looking quite pretty, like a stained-glass window.

directions

ROSE ENDS (make two)

The circle is worked in rnds. Rnds are joined with a sl st.

FOUNDATION

Using MC, ch 6. Join the ch with a sl st to form a ring.

FIRST LAYER OF PETALS

Rnd 1: ch 5 (counts as dc, ch 2), [dc, ch 2] 5 times, join rnd with a sl st to 3rd ch of ch 5 (you should have 6 ch spaces). Fasten off.

Rnd 2: using CC, ch 1, sc in top of same st where you joined the rnd, [work 5 dc in the next ch space, sc in next dc] 5 times, end with 5 dc in the last ch space, join to first sc with a sl st. Fasten off.

SECOND LAYER OF PETALS

Rnd 1: using MC, join yarn with a sl st, to the back (wrong) side of the sc where you just joined. (See "Pattern Notes".)

Sc in that loop. [Ch 5, sc in the back side of the next sc] 5 times, end with ch 5, join to the first sc with a sl st (6 ch spaces).

Rnd 2: ch 1, [(sc, work 7 tr, sc) all in the next ch space] 6 times. Join rnd with a sl st. Fasten off.

THIRD LAYER OF PETALS

Rnd 1: using CC, join yarn with a sl st, to the back (wrong) side of the sc where you just joined. (See "Pattern Notes" above.) Sc in that loop. [Ch 7, sc in the back side of the next sc] 5 times, end with ch 5, join to the first sc with a sl st (6 ch spaces).

Rnd 2: ch 1, [(sc, work 9 tr, sc) all in the next ch space] 6 times. Join rnd with a sl st. Fasten off.

PILLOW BODY

To k in the rnd, measure the circumference of your pillow form and CO the appropriate number of sts. For example, if your form is 20" around and you are knitting 4 sts to the inch, CO 80 sts.

Join rnd, being careful not to twist, and k until form is long enough to cover the entire bolster.

To k flat, measure the bolster lengthwise and CO the appropriate number of sts. Cont knitting until piece will wrap around the bolster with 1–2 extra rows for seaming.

finishing

Cover ends of bolster form with coordinating cotton fabric and tack down using thread. The Irish Rose crocheted ends have lots of lacy spaces, and without the fabric, you'll see the plain white (or other color) of your bolster form shining through. As long as the ends are covered, you're fine—don't worry about fancy stitching; this will all get covered up.

If you k your pillow cover in the rnd, pull it over the bolster form. If you k it flat, seam the ends, then pull it over.

Using yarn needle and coordinating yarn, st crocheted roses to either end of bolster.

hemp facecloth

BY KIMBERLY ALDERTON

Spurred on by yours truly, Kim tried knitting with hemp for the first time here. This facecloth is good and "scrubby" for when you'd like a little exfoliation, and it dries quickly due to the fingering-weight yarn and open laciness of the pattern. Hemp is durable, sturdy, and in the case of Hemp for Knitting's yarn, beautifully colored. It will stand up to many years of use and just gets nicer as it ages.

SIZE

One size fits all.

FINISHED MEASUREMENTS

Dimensions: 5" x 5"

MATERIALS

Hemp for Knitting #101 allhemp 3 (100% hemp; 165 yd/150 m per 50 g skein); color: Sprout; 1 skein

U.S. #6/4 mm needle of your choice (straight or circular)

GAUGE

Gauge is not critical to this project.

PATTERN NOTES

Hemp doesn't like to be torn out multiple times—it definitely tends to have a direction in terms of how you knit it, and reversing it makes the hemp unhappy. This pattern is so simple that the chance you'll need to rip out any stitches is slim!

If you've got a little hook near your sink, you might also like to crochet a chain or make an i-cord on one corner with which to hang up the cloth to dry.

directions

CO 39 sts.

K 5 rows.

BEGIN LACE PATTERN

Row 1: knit.

Row 2: k5 (this is your edging); *k2tog, yo*, rep from * to * until the last 6 sts; k1, yo, k5.

Rep rows 1 and 2 until the washcloth is the size of your dreams. Assuming, of course, you dream about such things.

K 5 rows.

BO and enjoy!

resource guide

alt fiber yarn sources

Blue Sky Alpacas—blueskyalpacas.com
Lovely organic cotton yarns, both hand- and mill-spun in a wide range of beautiful colors.

Classic Elite Yarns—classiceliteyarns.com
Bamboo in a brilliant range of colors, and more.

Foxfibre Naturally Colored Cotton—vreseis.com
See vreseis.com/sally_fox_story.htm for the full story of how Sally Vreseis Fox created her innovative line of colored cotton fibers, and see vreseis.com/colordeveloping.html for additional information on altering the color of these dyed-in-the-plant fibers using heat, pH, and so on.

Habu Textiles—habutextiles.com
Glorious specialty yarns from Japan and elsewhere, including some of the rarest and (until now) hardest-to-find alt fibers for handknitting and weaving. Order their sample book; it's well worth it to experience small amounts of each yarn without having to order a whole ball right away.

Handmaiden Yarns—handmaiden.ca
Source of the most lush, beautifully colored, hand-painted SeaCell blend yarns out there.

Kollage Yarns—kollageyarns.com
Cotton sock yarns and Cornucopia corn fiber yarns.

Lanaknits Designs/Hemp for Knitting—hempforknitting.com
The best hemp yarn available today, hands down. If there's anything better, I certainly haven't knit with it. Their hemp blends are equally luscious. These are the yarns used by Felicia for her dye examples on page 17. See their "About Us" page for a hilarious photograph of Lana "tenderizing" her earliest hemp yarns on a rock.

The Little Barn, Inc.—littlebarninc.com
Naturally colored cotton for spinning as well as some other unusual alt fibers for spinning such as recycled denim and soda bottles (it's softer than it sounds).

Louet—louet.com
Notably, Louet is one of the best sources of alt fiber spinning materials as well as yarns, featuring a wide selection of hemp, linen, organic cotton, and other materials. If you'd like to try your hand at spinning alt fibers, they're a great place to start.

Near Sea Naturals—nearseanaturals.com

Source of hand-spun nettle and banana yarn as well as alt fiber–based organic fabrics (make an organic hemp herringbone fabric skirt to match your Avery Jacket; see page 35).

South West Trading Company (SWTC)—soysilk.com

The ones who started it all: Jonelle Raffino and company are constantly working to bring more and more fantastic alt fiber yarns to the market, as well as spinning fibers and other products (if you want a soy fiber teddy bear, this is where to look).

SweetGeorgiaYarns—sweetgeorgiayarns.com

A collection of yarns and fibers from organic, sustainable, and renewable sources, "Supernatural SweetGeorgia" yarns are hand dyed with natural and plant dyes. Available in bamboo, silk, linen, organic cotton, organic wool, and other materials; a portion of profits are donated to environmental organizations.

Tilli Tomas—tillitomas.com

Elegant SeaCell and silk blends, plus pre-beaded silk ribbon yarn perfect for evening wear or just a little bit of glam for every day.

Universal Yarn Company—universalyarn.com

Bamboo, SeaCell, and many other alt fiber yarns.

order yarns online

These yarn stores and online shops carry a wide variety of the best alt fiber yarns. Most ship to both Canada and the United States and are staffed by knowledgeable yarn experts who can help you find the best yarn for your project.

- Kpixie—kpixie.com
- Lettuce Knit—lettuceknit.ca
- Luxe Fibre—luxefibre.com (Natasha Fialkov)
- The Sweet Sheep—thesweetsheep.ca
- SweetGeorgia Yarns—sweetgeorgiayarns.com (Felicia Lo)
- Threadbear Fiber Arts—threadbearfiberarts.com
- WEBS—yarn.com

Need additional help? The author's shop, Stitch Cleveland, can also help you find the right yarns—stitchcleveland.com

suggested references

BOOKS

Barber, Elizabeth Wayland. 1995. *Women's Work: The First 20,000 Years—Women, Cloth and Society in Early Times*. New York: W.W. Norton & Company.

Bessette, Arleen R. 2001. *The Rainbow beneath My Feet: A Mushroom Dyer's Field Guide*. Syracuse, NY: Syracuse University Press.

Buchanan, Rita. 1995. *A Dyer's Garden: From Plant to Pot, Growing Dyes for Natural Fibers*. Loveland, CO: Interweave

Press. If you're a gardener or know someone who is, you can grow many dyestuffs at home with little effort!

Casselman, Karen Diadick. 2001. *Lichen Dyes: The New Source Book*. Mineola, NY: Dover Publications. The best book available on this esoteric yet fascinating topic.

Casselman, Karen Leigh. 1993. *Craft of the Dyer: Colour from Plants and Lichens*. Mineola, NY: Dover Publications.

Kroll, Carol. 1981. *The Whole Craft of Spinning: From the Raw Material to the Finished Yarn*. Mineola, NY: Dover Publications. Chapter 8 contains much information on spinning alt fibers, including milkweed, cattail, dandelion fluff, and more.

Liles, J. N. 1990. *The Art and Craft of Natural Dyeing: Traditional Recipes for Modern Use*. Knoxville, TN: University of Tennessee Press.

Parkes, Clara. 2007. *The Knitter's Book of Yarn: The Ultimate Guide to Choosing, Using and Enjoying Yarn*. New York: Potter Craft.

Richards, Lynne, and Ronald J. Tyrl. 2005. *Dyes from American Native Plants: A Practical Guide*. Portland, OR: Timber Press.

Singer, Amy R. 2007. *No Sheep for You: Knit Happy with Cotton, Silk, Linen, Hemp, Bamboo and Other Delights*. Loveland, CO: Interweave Press.

van Stralen, Trudy. 1994. *Indigo, Madder & Marigold: A Portfolio of Colors from Natural Dyes*. Loveland, CO: Interweave Press. Trudy van Stralen and her family run Louet North America (see "Alt Fiber Yarn Sources" above); you can also buy this book online through their website.

Vogue Knitting Magazine. 2006. *The Vogue Knitting Stitchionary—Volume 2: Cables*. New York: Sixth&Spring Books.

Wipplinger, Michele. [2002] 2005. *Natural Dye Instruction Booklet: Everything You Need to Know about Dyeing and Painting with Natural Dye Extracts*. Seattle, WA: Earthues. Available from Earthues (see "Natural Dye Supplies" below).

ONLINE AND MAGAZINE ARTICLES

Article on dyeing alt fibers by Jonelle Raffino of South West Trading Company: http://soysilk.com/images/Dyeing_SWTC_article.jpg

Article on dyeing with herbs and other plants: http://crafty herbalknitter.com/blog/

Article on nonwool sock yarns by popular knitblogger Grumperina: http://www.grumperina.com/knitblog/non woolysockyarn.htm

Article on spinning milkweed by Carol Johnson Collins and Elizabeth Dyak, "Milkweed Stalk Fiber." *Spin Off* (Winter 2003). Back issues available from interweave.com.

Article on traditional banana-cloth manufacturing: http://www.japanupdate.com/?id=4103

"Plant Freak" article referenced in the "Introduction" (page 3): http://www.knitty.com/ISSUEsummer04/FEATplantfreak.html

natural dye supplies

Earthues, Maiwa Handprints, and Dharma Trading Company are three of the best suppliers of reliable natural dye materials. Earthues sells smaller quantities of its natural dye powders through a large network of suppliers—see the "Where to Buy" page on the website—but its color collections, which comprise everything you might need to start dyeing in one box, are a great way to get started. Maiwa sells various natural dye materials directly through the "Craft Supply" section of its website; it is located in Canada, if you're north of the border, and it has excellent directions for mordanting and other dyeing information on its website. Dharma Trading Company stocks dye remover, fabric blanks, and other useful items as well as the dye! All three companies pursue environmentally responsible business practices, spread knowledge about dyeing and other fiber-related arts, and contribute to their communities in a number of ways. This is another reason to support them, apart from their quality products.

Dharma Trading Company
1604 Fourth St.
San Rafael, CA 94901
(800) 542-5227
dharmatrading.com

**Earthues: A Natural
Color Company**
5129 Ballard Ave. NW
Seattle, WA 98107
(206) 789-1065
earthues.com

Maiwa Handprints Ltd.
6-1666 Johnson St.
Granville Island
Vancouver, BC V6H 3S2
(604) 669-3939
maiwa.com

other dye supplies and information

ProChemical is an excellent source of all different types of dye. It offers a tech-support line separate from the orders department. Chances are if you're having a problem with one of ProChemical's dyes, tech support will know how to fix it! The company also stocks a full line of dye auxiliaries such as mordants and Synthropol (an artificial *wetting* agent often used in dyeing to prepare fibers to accept color). The website is an excellent resource for dyeing information, offering directions for just about every process you can imagine, from straight immersion dyeing to soy wax batik.

ProChemical & Dye
P.O. Box 14
Somerset, MA 02726
Orders: (800) 228-9393
Customer service and technical issues: (508) 676-3838

about the designers

KIMBERLY ALDERTON (Hemp Facecloth) has an alarming habit of adopting balls of yarn. One particular favorite is named Bruce, and it gets the same loving strokes as her pug army does. Really, I'm not kidding. Remarkably, the pug army leaves the pet yarn balls alone to multiply exponentially in Kimberly's Cleveland, Ohio, home.

LAURA CHAU (Avery Jacket) just received her bachelor's degree in science from the University of Toronto and is trying to make it as a professional knitter. She is the author of *Teach Yourself VISUALLY Sock Knitting* (John Wiley & Sons, 2008) and her designs can be found on the pages of Knitty.com. Laura knits, spins, dyes, teaches, and sells yarn in Toronto, Ontario. You can find her at cosmicpluto.com.

TAMARA DEL SONNO (Audrey Swing Coat, Bamboo Cardigan Trio, and Pure Cables Cardigan Set) has been knitting since she coerced her mom to teach her how at the age of eight. She took on her first student at the ripe old age of twelve. While at university, Tamara studied clothing and textiles; she loves color and texture. She has worked at the Yarn Loft in Del Mar, California, and at several shops in Minnesota, including Clickity Sticks & Yarns and the Yarn Garage. Tamara's award-winning designs can be found in *101 One-Skein Wonders* (Storey Publishing, 2006), *101 Designer One-Skein Wonders* (Storey Publishing, 2007), a *Stitch 'n Bitch* calendar, and at ClickitySticks.com.

AMY GUMM (De Fleur Socks) is a habitual sock knitter who blogs at iheartknitting.com.

SIVIA HARDING (Midnight Lace Stole) is a designer who dabbles in lace, beads, and, most recently, socks. She has been self-publishing her knitting patterns for several years, and her work can be seen featured in the online magazine Knitty, the Australian print magazine *Yarn*, and the books *Knitgrrl 2* (Watson Guptill Publications, 2006), *Big Girl Knits* (Potter Craft, 2006), and *No Sheep for You* (Interweave Press, 2007). You can follow her knitting adventures on her blog at www.siviaharding.blogspot.com and in her groups on Yahoo and Ravelry. Her patterns are for sale on her website (www.siviaharding.com) and at numerous yarn stores.

EMMA JANE HOGBIN (Clever Socks) is a Canadian Internet consultant. She likes her Scotch peaty, her rabbits angora, and her antihistamines in shades of blue. She chronicles her life at www.emmajane.net.

JULIE ARMSTRONG HOLETZ (Kenaf Spike-Stitch Bag) is the author of *Uncommon Crochet* (Ten Speed Press, 2008). She's worked with me on a number of projects now, and always does lovely things like send lollipop valentines after the project is finished. Julie likes to cruise yarn shops in Seattle, design crochet patterns, and teach fiber arts to the kids in her neighborhood; she dislikes Brussels sprouts and ribbon yarns. She writes about yarn and more at skamama. com.

AMY O'NEILL HOUCK (Irish Rose Bolster) is a writer and a crochet and knitwear designer. Her grandmother taught her how to crochet when Amy was eight years old, and she's been crocheting every since. Amy is the author of *The Color Book of Felted Crochet* (Home Arts, 2008) with designer Stina Ramos, and of the forthcoming *Knits for Bears to Wear* (Potter Craft, 2008). She has been a guest on the DIY Network's *Knitty Gritty*, and she writes about crochet technique, history, and fashion for *Crochet Today* and *Interweave Crochet*. Amy recently moved to Cordova, Alaska, where she makes the most of her woolly stash.

KATE JACKSON (Fern Tee and Phoenix Quick Wrap) is the designer of Kate Jackson Knits patterns, which are available in your LYS and online. Her designs have been featured in several books and magazines, including *Knitscene* and *Vogue Knitting*. She owns Knitting on the Square (knitting onthesquare.com), a yarn shop in Chardon, Ohio, and can be found online at www.katejacksonknits.com.

FELICIA LO (see information on natural dyeing, page 16) is driven by an obsessive, passionate, and often tumultuous relationship with color. The dyer and owner of SweetGeorgia Yarns, a hand-painted yarn company based in Vancouver, Felicia designs and creates luxurious textiles and textile products. Founded in 2005, SweetGeorgia Yarns produces intense, relentless, and unapologetic color—sometimes irreverent and fierce, sometimes bubbly and saccharine sweet, and always exquisitely appealing. Felicia has been exploring new fibers and natural dyeing, and blogs about her dyeing, weaving, spinning, and knitting experiences at http://blog.sweetgeorgiayarns.com.

NIKOL LOHR (Linen-Times-Two Skirt) is the author of *Naughty Needles: Sexy, Saucy Knits for the Bedroom and Beyond* (Potter Craft, 2006) and the genius behind The Harveyville Project (harveyvilleproject.com), an art residency program housed in an old rural Kansas schoolhouse where Yarn School and Felt School are held. She writes about knitting and her constant battle against stash at thriftyknitter.com.

JILLIAN MORENO (Fuji Table Set) is the coauthor of *Big Girl Knits* and *More Big Girl Knits* (Potter Craft, 2006 and 2008, respectively) with Amy R. Singer, and the designer of a new line of curvy-girl knit patterns for Classic Elite Yarns. She's the editor of *KnittySpin* and a totally self-taught designer. She hates rules. She firmly believes that if you obsess about something for long enough, you will figure out how to do it. She also believes in excessive chocolate and that girls who knit will grow up to rule the world. She lives in Ann Arbor, Michigan, with her husband, two kids, and way too much yarn.

ANDI SMITH (Summer Pine Shawl, Sjaal Scarf, ZenLuv Socks, Love-Squared Gauntlets, Sunny-Side-Up Socks, and Rose Kilim Sweater) has been working with yarn for more years than she can count. She has a hard time deciding whether simple or complex designs are her favorite; however, from the number of works in progress she has, it's fair to say that she is thoroughly exploring all possibilities. She can be found online at knitbrit.com.

JENNY WILLEY (Bow Tank), crocheter extraordinaire, finally learned to knit three years ago after many trials and tribulations. She conquered beginning knitting with the most unlikely of projects—socks! Jenny knits in Minneapolis, which is cold, but not nearly as cold as you think.

KERI WILLIAMS (Merian Wrap) started knitting a long time ago and hasn't really stopped since. Having lived in a number of places, from Great Britain to New Zealand, she now lives in Toronto, Canada, with her husband, Mike. She collects wool; he collects science fiction books. Eventually, they will have to buy a bigger house.

about the author

SHANNON OKEY (Rose Kilim Sweater, Dutch Girl Head-scarf, Sea Creature Möbius Necklet, and Irish Rose Bolster) writes. A lot. Come on, look at the "Also by . . ." list. When she's not tied to her laptop, she's knitting, spinning, dyeing, felting, or doing any number of other fibery arts. She writes a column for *knit.1* magazine; is a frequent contributor to magazines such as *CRAFT* and *Yarn Market News*; has appeared on crafty television shows, including *Knitty Gritty*, *Uncommon Threads*, and *Crafters Coast to Coast*; and teaches all over the country. She co-owns a studio workshop/store called Stitch Cleveland (stitchcleveland.com) and created Stitch Cooperative, a designer-owned pattern distribution network. In her spare time, she helps other creative professionals publish their own books, do PR, and build websites. In case you haven't quite guessed it, Shannon works way too much. But she loves it, and that's all that matters. Shannon lives in Cleveland, Ohio, with her eternally patient boyfriend, Tamas Jakab, two naughty cats, Spike and Giles, and a dachshund princess named Anezka. You can find Shannon at knitgrrl.com.

ALSO BY SHANNON OKEY

Knitgrrl (Watson Guptill Publications, 2005)
Knitgrrl 2 (Watson Guptill Publications, 2006)
Spin to Knit (Interweave Press, 2006)
Crochet Style (Creative Homeowner, 2007)
Felt Frenzy (with Heather Brack, Interweave Press, 2007)
Just Socks (editor, Potter Craft, 2007)
Just Gifts (editor, Potter Craft, 2007)
AlterNation (with Alexandra Underhill, North Light, 2007)
The Pillow Book (Chronicle Books, 2008)
How to Knit in the Woods (Skipstone, 2008)

FEEDBACK, QUESTIONS, ERRATA

Check out author Shannon Okey's website at knitgrrl.com for the latest pattern updates, yarn information, podcasts, and more.

index

A

Abaca, 7
Achiote, 18
Acrylic, 5
Agave, 4, 8, 11–12
Alderton, Kimberly, 110
Allo or Alloo, 10
Alt fiber yarns, 1–2, 4
   availability of, 7
   blocking and finishing, 6–7
   direction of, 6
   dyeing, 13–15
   handbook on, 7–9
   sources of, 106
   synthetic, 5
Aluminum acetate, 17
American nettle, 12
Annatto, 18
Audrey Swing Coat, 30–33
Aveda, 18
Avery Jacket, 34–39

B

Bag, Kenaf Spike-Stitch, 95–98
Ball winder, 6
Bamboo, 5, 7
   Audrey Swing Coat, 30–33
   Bamboo Cardigan Trio, 45 50
   Bow Tank, 43–45
Banana, 12
Barber, Wayland, 14
Bashofu (banana cloth), 12
Bast fibers, processing, 4–5
Beaded knitting, Midnight Lace Stole,
   56–63
Blue, 16
Blue Sky Alpacas, 106
Boll, 5
Bordhi, Cat, 66
Bow Tank, 43–45
Brazilwood, 18
Buchanan, Rita, 19

C

Cabuya, 8
Cardigan. *See* Sweaters
Casselman, Karen Diadick, 15
Cattail, 11, 12
Cellulose-based lyocell, 1
Center-pull balls, 6

Chau, Laura, 110
Classic Elite Yans, 106
Clever Socks, 92 94
Coat, Audrey Swing, 30–33
Cochineal, 18–19
Color, 13, 16, 18–19
Corn fiber, 2, 5, 8
   De Fleur Socks, 80–85
   Fern Tee, 40–42
Cotton, 1, 5
   growing, 2
   organic, 10, 14
   Rose Kilim Sweater, 14, 15, 19,
      26–29
   Sunny-Side-Up Socks, 86–88
   ZenLuv Socks, 89–91
Craft yarn, 12

D

Dandelion fluff, 11
De Fleur Socks, 80–85
Del Sonno, Tamara, 110
Dental-floss threaders, 57
Dharma Trading Company, 109
Dutch Girl Headscarf, 78–79

Dyed in the wool, 13, 14
A Dyer's Garden (Buchanan), 19
Dyer's rocket, 18

E

Earthues: A Natural Color
    Company, 109

F

Facecloth, hemp, 104–5
Fair Isle pattern, 72–73, 75
Fern Tee, 8, 40–42
Fique, 8
Flax, 2
Floss, 12
Fox, Sally Vreseis, 14
Foxfibre, 14
Foxfibre Naturally Colored Cotton, 106
Fuji Table Set, 8, 98–100

G

Gauntlets, Love-Squared, 74–77
Gumm, Amy, 110

H

Habu Textiles, 6, 7, 70, 106
Hand-dyed yarn, leaking of color
    and, 27
Handmaiden Yarns, 10, 11, 106
Hand warmers, 74–77

Harding, Sivia, 110
Headscarf, Dutch Girl, 78–79
Hemp, 2, 5, 8
    Avery Jacket, 34–39
    facecloth, 104–5
Henna, 18
Hogbin, Emma Jane, 110
Holetz, Julie Armstrong, 95, 111
Houck, Amy O'Neill, 111
Howell, Vickie, 30, 43

I

Indigo, 14, 16, 18
Ingeo, 8
Irish Rose Bolster, 101–3

J

Jacket, Avery, 34–39
Jackson, Kate, 111

K

Kapok, 5, 12, 13
Kenaf, 2, 8
    Kenaf Spike-Stitch Bag, 95–98
Kenaf Spike-Stitch Bag, 95–98
The Knitter's Book of Yarn (Parkes), 5
Knitty.com, 3
Kollage Yarns, 106
Kroll, Carol, 11

L

Lac, 18
Lanaknits Designs / Hemp for
    Knitting, 106
Lichen Dyes: The New Source Book
    (Casselman), 15
Linen, 1, 4, 9, 24
    Fuji Table Set, 98–100
    Linen-Times-Two Skirt, 22–25
Lion Brand, 14, 19
The Little Barn, Inc., 14, 106
Lo, Felicia, 15, 111
Lohr, Nikol, 111
Louet, 106
Love-Squared Gauntlets, 74–77
Lycra, 4
Lyocell, 9–10

M

Madder root, 15, 18
Maiwa Handprints Ltd., 109
Manila hemp, 7
Marigold dye, 18
Merian Wrap, 64–65
Microfibers, 5
Midnight Lace Stole, 56–63
Milk fiber, 12
Milkweed, 5, 11, 12–13
Möbius strips, 66
Modal, 10

Monkey balls, 18
Monkey brains, 18
Mordanting, 17, 19
Moreno, Jillian, 98, 111–12

N

Natural colors, 13–15
Natural dyes, 16, 18–19, 109
Natural dyestuffs, 14
Near Sea Naturals, 107
Necklet, Sea Creature Möbius, 66–67
Nettles, 2, 10
New, Debbie, 64
*No Sheep for You: Knit Happy with
     Cotton, Silk, Linen, Hemp,
     Bamboo and Other Delights*
     (Singer), 3

O

Okey, Shannon, 113
Organic cotton, 10, 14
Osage orange, 18
Overdyeing, 16

P

Parkes, Clara, 5
Phoenix Quick Wrap, 68–69
Pillows, Irish Rose Bolster, 101–3
Pineapple, 1–2, 10
Pine ribbon, 6

Pinks, 18
Plant-based yarns, 1–2
Polyester, 5
ProChemical, 109
Pure Cables Cardigan Set, 51–55
Purples, 18

Q

Qualities of yarn, 3–5
Quebracho, 18

R

Raffino, Jonelle, 2, 12
Ramie, 2, 4, 10
Red dyes, 18
Retting process, 9
Rose Kilim Sweater, 14, 15, 19, 26–29

S

Sandalwood, 18
Scarf, Sjaal, 72–73
Scribble lace, 64
Scrunch test, 23
Scutching, 9
Seacell, 10
Sea Creature Möbius Necklet, 66–67
Seaweed-based fibers, 5
Shawl, Summer Pine, 70–71
Short-stapled fibers, 5
Silk, 11, 12

Silk floss tree, 12
Singer, Amy R., 2–3
Sisal, 11–12
Sizing, 6, 70–71
Sjaal Scarf, 72–73
Skirts
     Bamboo Cardigan, 45, 50
     Linen-Times-Two, 22–25
Smartfiber AG, 10
Smith, Andi, 112
Socks
     Clever, 92–94
     De Fleur, 80–85
     Sunny-Side-Up, 86–88
     ZenLuv, 89–91
South West Trading Company
     (SWTC), 2, 7, 11, 12, 107
Soy, 1, 2, 5, 11
     Pure Cables Cardigan Set, 51–55
SoySilk, 2, 11
     Phoenix Quick Wrap, 68–69
Spin to Knit (Okey), 11, 15
Staple length, 9–11
Stole, Midnight Lace, 56–63
Summer Pine Shawl, 6, 70–71
Sunny-Side-Up Socks, 86–88
Sweaters
     Bamboo Cardigan Trio, 45, 48–49
     Pure Cables Cardigan Set, 51–55
     Rose Kilim, 14, 15, 19, 26–29

SweetGeorgia Yarns, 15, 107
Synthetic alt fiber yarns, 5

T

Table Set, Fuji, 8, 98–100
Tank
    Bamboo Cardigan Trio, 45, 46–48
    Bow, 43–45
Tannin, 17
Tee, Fern, 40–42
Tencel, 1, 9
Theaker, Julie, 3
Tilli Tomas, 107
Tow, 9
Treasures of Magical Knitting
        (Bordhi), 66

U

Uncommon Crochet (Holetz), 95
Universal Yarn Company, 107
Uruku, 18

V

Vogue Knitting Stitchionary—
        Volume 2: Cables, 27

W

Washing soda, 14
Weld, 16, 18
The Whole Craft of Spinning (Kroll), 11

Willey, Jenny, 112
Williams, Keri, 112
Woad, 16
Women's Work: The First 20,000 Years
        (Barber), 14
Wood pulp, 1
Wool, advantage of, over alt fibers, 4
Wraps
    Merian, 64–65
    Phoenix Quick, 68–69

X

Xylem, 4

Y

Yarndex.com, 7
Yarns
    availability of, 7
    choosing and knitting the right
        way, 5–6
    ordering online, 107
    qualities of, 3–5
Yellows, 16
Yucca, 4

Z

ZenLuv Socks, 89–91